interchange
FIFTH EDITION

Student's Book

Jack C. Richards
with Jonathan Hull and Susan Proctor

2

WITH EBOOK

CAMBRIDGE
UNIVERSITY PRESS

CAMBRIDGE
UNIVERSITY PRESS

University Printing House, Cambridge CB2 8BS, United Kingdom

One Liberty Plaza, 20th Floor, New York, NY 10006, USA

477 Williamstown Road, Port Melbourne, VIC 3207, Australia

314–321, 3rd Floor, Plot 3, Splendor Forum, Jasola District Centre, New Delhi – 110025, India

103 Penang Road, #05-06/07, Visioncrest Commercial, Singapore 238467

Cambridge University Press is part of the University of Cambridge.

It furthers the University's mission by disseminating knowledge in the pursuit of education, learning and research at the highest international levels of excellence.

www.cambridge.org
Information on this title: www.cambridge.org/9781009040495

© Cambridge University Press 1991, 2017

This publication is in copyright. Subject to statutory exception and to the provisions of relevant collective licensing agreements, no reproduction of any part may take place without the written permission of Cambridge University Press.

First published 1991
Second edition 2000
Third edition 2005
Fourth edition 2013
Fifth edition 2017
Fifth edition update published 2021

20 19 18

Printed in Malaysia by Vivar Printing

A catalogue record for this publication is available from the British Library

ISBN 978-1-009-04049-5 Student's Book 2 with eBook
ISBN 978-1-009-04050-1 Student's Book 2A with eBook
ISBN 978-1-009-04051-8 Student's Book 2B with eBook
ISBN 978-1-009-04069-3 Student's Book 2 with Digital Pack
ISBN 978-1-009-04070-9 Student's Book 2A with Digital Pack
ISBN 978-1-009-04071-6 Student's Book 2B with Digital Pack
ISBN 978-1-316-62269-8 Workbook 2
ISBN 978-1-316-62270-4 Workbook 2A
ISBN 978-1-316-62271-1 Workbook 2B
ISBN 978-1-108-40709-0 Teacher's Edition 2
ISBN 978-1-316-62228-5 Class Audio 2
ISBN 978-1-009-04072-3 Full Contact 2 with Digital Pack
ISBN 978-1-009-04073-0 Full Contact 2A with Digital Pack
ISBN 978-1-009-04074-7 Full Contact 2B with Digital Pack
ISBN 978-1-108-40306-1 Presentation Plus 2

Additional resources for this publication at cambridgeone.org

Cambridge University Press has no responsibility for the persistence or accuracy of URLs for external or third-party internet websites referred to in this publication, and does not guarantee that any content on such websites is, or will remain, accurate or appropriate. Information regarding prices, travel timetables, and other factual information given in this work is correct at the time of first printing but Cambridge University Press does not guarantee the accuracy of such information thereafter.

Informed by teachers

Teachers from all over the world helped develop *Interchange Fifth Edition*. They looked at everything – from the color of the designs to the topics in the conversations – in order to make sure that this course will work in the classroom. We heard from 1,500 teachers in:

- Surveys
- Focus Groups
- In-Depth Reviews

We appreciate the help and input from everyone. In particular, we'd like to give the following people our special thanks:

Jader Franceschi, **Actúa Idiomas,** Bento Gonçalves, Rio Grande do Sul, Brazil

Juliana Dos Santos Voltan Costa, **Actus Idiomas,** São Paulo, Brazil

Ella Osorio, **Angelo State University,** San Angelo, TX, US

Mary Hunter, **Angelo State University,** San Angelo, TX, US

Mario César González, **Angloamericano de Monterrey, SC,** Monterrey, Mexico

Samantha Shipman, **Auburn High School,** Auburn, AL, US

Linda, **Bernick Language School,** Radford, VA, US

Dave Lowrance, **Bethesda University of California,** Yorba Linda, CA, US

Tajbakhsh Hosseini, **Bezmialem Vakif University,** Istanbul, Turkey

Dilek Gercek, **Bil English,** Izmir, Turkey

Erkan Kolat, **Biruni University, ELT,** Istanbul, Turkey

Nika Gutkowska, **Bluedata International,** New York, NY, US

Daniel Alcocer Gómez, **Cecati 92,** Guadalupe, Nuevo León, Mexico

Samantha Webb, **Central Middle School,** Milton-Freewater, OR, US

Verónica Salgado, **Centro Anglo Americano,** Cuernavaca, Mexico

Ana Rivadeneira Martínez and Georgia P. de Machuca, **Centro de Educación Continua – Universidad Politécnica del Ecuador,** Quito, Ecuador

Anderson Francisco Guimerães Maia, **Centro Cultural Brasil Estados Unidos,** Belém, Brazil

Rosana Mariano, **Centro Paula Souza,** São Paulo, Brazil

Carlos de la Paz Arroyo, Teresa Noemí Parra Alarcón, Gilberto Bastida Gaytan, Manuel Esquivel Román, and Rosa Cepeda Tapia, **Centro Universitario Angloamericano,** Cuernavaca, Morelos, Mexico

Antonio Almeida, **CETEC,** Morelos, Mexico

Cinthia Ferreira, **Cinthia Ferreira Languages Services,** Toronto, ON, Canada

Phil Thomas and Sérgio Sanchez, **CLS Canadian Language School,** São Paulo, Brazil

Celia Concannon, **Cochise College,** Nogales, AZ, US

Maria do Carmo Rocha and CAOP English team, **Colégio Arquidiocesano Ouro Preto – Unidade Cônego Paulo Dilascio,** Ouro Preto, Brazil

Kim Rodriguez, **College of Charleston North,** Charleston, SC, US

Jesús Leza Alvarado, **Coparmex English Institute,** Monterrey, Mexico

John Partain, **Cortazar,** Guanajuato, Mexico

Alexander Palencia Navas, **Cursos de Lenguas, Universidad del Atlántico,** Barranquilla, Colombia

Kenneth Johan Gerardo Steenhuisen Cera, Melfi Osvaldo Guzman Triana, and Carlos Alberto Algarín Jiminez, **Cursos de Lenguas Extranjeras Universidad del Atlantico,** Barranquilla, Colombia

Jane P Kerford, **East Los Angeles College,** Pasadena, CA, US

Daniela, **East Village,** Campinas, São Paulo, Brazil

Rosalva Camacho Orduño, **Easy English for Groups S.A. de C.V.,** Monterrey, Nuevo León, Mexico

Adonis Gimenez Fusetti, **Easy Way Idiomas,** Ibiúna, Brazil

Eileen Thompson, **Edison Community College,** Piqua, OH, US

Ahminne Handeri O.L Froede, **Englishouse escola de idiomas,** Teófilo Otoni, Brazil

Ana Luz Delgado-Izazola, **Escuela Nacional Preparatoria 5, UNAM,** Mexico City, Mexico

Nancy Alarcón Mendoza, **Facultad de Estudios Superiores Zaragoza, UNAM,** Mexico City, Mexico

Marcilio N. Barros, **Fast English USA,** Campinas, São Paulo, Brazil

Greta Douthat, **FCI Ashland,** Ashland, KY, US

Carlos Lizárraga González, **Grupo Educativo Anglo Americano, S.C.,** Mexico City, Mexico

Hugo Fernando Alcántar Valle, **Instituto Politécnico Nacional, Escuela Superior de Comercio y Administración-Unidad Santotomás, Celex Esca Santo Tomás,** Mexico City, Mexico

Sueli Nascimento, **Instituto Superior de Educação do Rio de Janeiro,** Rio de Janeiro, Brazil

Elsa F Monteverde, **International Academic Services,** Miami, FL, US

Laura Anand, **Irvine Adult School,** Irvine, CA, US

Prof. Marli T. Fernandes (principal) and Prof. Dr. Jefferson J. Fernandes (pedagogue), **Jefferson Idiomass,** São Paulo, Brazil

Herman Bartelen, **Kanda Gaigo Gakuin,** Tokyo, Japan

Cassia Silva, **Key Languages,** Key Biscayne, FL, US

Sister Mary Hope, **Kyoto Notre Dame Joshi Gakuin,** Kyoto, Japan

Nate Freedman, **LAL Language Centres,** Boston, MA, US

Richard Janzen, **Langley Secondary School,** Abbotsford, BC, Canada

Christina Abel Gabardo, **Language House,** Campo Largo, Brazil

Ivonne Castro, **Learn English International,** Cali, Colombia

Julio Cesar Maciel Rodrigues, **Liberty Centro de Línguas,** São Paulo, Brazil

Ann Gibson, **Maynard High School,** Maynard, MA, US

Martin Darling, **Meiji Gakuin Daigaku,** Tokyo, Japan

Dax Thomas, **Meiji Gakuin Daigaku,** Yokohama, Kanagawa, Japan

Derya Budak, **Mevlana University,** Konya, Turkey

B Sullivan, **Miami Valley Career Technical Center International Program,** Dayton, OH, US

Julio Velazquez, **Milo Language Center,** Weston, FL, US

Daiane Siqueira da Silva, Luiz Carlos Buontempo, Marlete Avelina de Oliveira Cunha, Marcos Paulo Segatti, Morgana Eveline de Oliveira, Nadia Lia Gino Alo, and Paul Hyde Budgen, **New Interchange-Escola de Idiomas,** São Paulo, Brazil

Patrícia França Furtado da Costa, Juiz de Fora, Brazil

Patricia Servín

Chris Pollard, **North West Regional College SK,** North Battleford, SK, Canada

Olga Amy, **Notre Dame High School,** Red Deer, Canada

Amy Garrett, **Ouachita Baptist University,** Arkadelphia, AR, US

Mervin Curry, **Palm Beach State College,** Boca Raton, FL, US

Julie Barros, **Quality English Studio,** Guarulhos, São Paulo, Brazil

Teodoro González Saldaña and Jesús Monserrrta Mata Franco, **Race Idiomas,** Mexico City, Mexico

Autumn Westphal and Noga La`or, **Rennert International,** New York, NY, US

Antonio Gallo and Javy Palau, **Rigby Idiomas,** Monterrey, Mexico Tatiane Gabriela Sperb do Nascimento, **Right Way,** Igrejinha, Brazil

Mustafa Akgül, **Selahaddin Eyyubi Universitesi,** Diyarbakır, Turkey

James Drury M. Fonseca, **Senac Idiomas Fortaleza,** Fortaleza, Ceara, Brazil

Manoel Fialho S Neto, **Senac – PE,** Recife, Brazil

Jane Imber, **Small World,** Lawrence, KS, US

Tony Torres, **South Texas College,** McAllen, TX, US

Janet Rose, **Tennessee Foreign Language Institute,** College Grove, TN, US

Todd Enslen, **Tohoku University,** Sendai, Miyagi, Japan

Daniel Murray, **Torrance Adult School,** Torrance, CA, US

Juan Manuel Pulido Mendoza, **Universidad del Atlántico,** Barranquilla, Colombia

Juan Carlos Vargas Millán, **Universidad Libre Seccional Cali,** Cali (Valle del Cauca), Colombia

Carmen Cecilia Llanos Ospina, **Universidad Libre Seccional Cali,** Cali, Colombia

Jorge Noriega Zenteno, **Universidad Politécnica del Valle de México,** Estado de México, Mexico

Aimee Natasha Holguin S., **Universidad Politécnica del Valle de México UPVM,** Tultitlàn Estado de México, Mexico

Christian Selene Bernal Barraza, **UPVM Universidad Politécnica del Valle de México,** Ecatepec, Mexico

Lizeth Ramos Acosta, **Universidad Santiago de Cali,** Cali, Colombia

Silvana Dushku, **University of Illinois Champaign,** IL, US

Deirdre McMurtry, **University of Nebraska – Omaha,** Omaha, NE, US

Jason E Mower, **University of Utah,** Salt Lake City, UT, US

Paul Chugg, **Vanguard Taylor Language Institute,** Edmonton, Alberta, Canada

Henry Mulak, **Varsity Tutors,** Los Angeles, CA, US

Shirlei Strucker Calgaro and Hugo Guilherme Karrer, **VIP Centro de Idiomas,** Panambi, Rio Grande do Sul, Brazil

Eleanor Kelly, **Waseda Daigaku Extension Centre,** Tokyo, Japan

Sherry Ashworth, **Wichita State University,** Wichita, KS, US

Laine Bourdene, **William Carey University,** Hattiesburg, MS, US

Serap Aydın, Istanbul, Turkey

Liliana Covino, Guarulhos, Brazil

Yannuarys Jiménez, Barranquilla, Colombia

Juliana Morais Pazzini, Toronto, ON, Canada

Marlon Sanches, Montreal, Canada

Additional content contributed by Kenna Bourke, Inara Couto, Nic Harris, Greg Manin, Ashleigh Martinez, Laura McKenzie, Paul McIntyre, Clara Prado, Lynne Robertson, Mari Vargo, Theo Walker, and Maria Lucia Zaorob.

Classroom Language Student questions

I'll be Student A.

Which role are you going to take?

Can I borrow your . . . ?

Who wants to go first?

I'll go first.

Whose turn is it?

It's your turn.

Ready?

Yes, I am.

No, not yet.

Let's change roles and do it again.

OK.

Classroom Language

Plan of Book 2

Titles/Topics	Speaking	Grammar
UNIT 1 — PAGES 2–7 **Good memories** People; childhood; memories	Introducing yourself; talking about yourself; exchanging personal information; remembering your childhood; asking about someone's childhood	Past tense; *used to* for habitual actions
UNIT 2 — PAGES 8–13 **Life in the city** Transportation; transportation problems; city services	Talking about transportation and transportation problems; evaluating city services; asking for and giving information	Expressions of quantity with count and noncount nouns: *too many, too much, fewer, less, more, not enough*; indirect questions from Wh-questions
PROGRESS CHECK — PAGES 14–15		
UNIT 3 — PAGES 16–21 **Making changes** Houses and apartments; lifestyle changes; wishes	Describing positive and negative features; making comparisons; talking about lifestyle changes; expressing wishes	Evaluations and comparisons with adjectives: *not . . . enough, too, (not) as . . . as*; evaluations and comparisons with nouns: *not enough . . . , too much/many . . . , (not) as much/many . . . as*; *wish*
UNIT 4 — PAGES 22–27 **Have you ever tried it?** Food; recipes; cooking instructions; cooking methods	Talking about food; expressing likes and dislikes; describing a favorite snack; giving step-by-step instructions	Simple past vs. present perfect; sequence adverbs: *first, then, next, after that, finally*
PROGRESS CHECK — PAGES 28–29		
UNIT 5 — PAGES 30–35 **Hit the road!** Travel; vacations; plans	Describing vacation plans; giving travel advice; planning a vacation	Future with *be going to* and *will*; modals for necessity and suggestion: *must, need to, (don't) have to, ought to, -'d better, should (not)*
UNIT 6 — PAGES 36–41 **Sure! I'll do it.** Complaints; household chores; requests; excuses; apologies	Making requests; agreeing to and refusing requests; complaining; apologizing; giving excuses	Two-part verbs; *will* for responding to requests; requests with modals and *Would you mind . . . ?*
PROGRESS CHECK — PAGES 42–43		
UNIT 7 — PAGES 44–49 **What do you use this for?** Technology; instructions	Describing technology; giving instructions; giving suggestions	Infinitives and gerunds for uses and purposes; imperatives and infinitives for giving suggestions
UNIT 8 — PAGES 50–55 **Time to celebrate!** Holidays; festivals; customs; celebrations	Describing holidays, festivals, customs, and special events	Relative clauses of time; adverbial clauses of time: *when, after, before*
PROGRESS CHECK — PAGES 56–57		

Pronunciation/Listening	Writing/Reading	Interchange Activity
Reduced form of *used to* Listening to people talk about their past	Writing a paragraph about your childhood "A Life in Paintings: The Frida Kahlo Story": Reading about the life of this Mexican painter	"We have a lot in common.": Finding out about a classmate's childhood **PAGE 114**
Syllable stress Listening to a description of a transportation system	Writing an online post on a community message board about a local issue "The World's Happiest Cities": Reading about the happiest cities in the world	"Top travel destinations": Suggesting ways to attract tourists to a city **PAGE 115**
Unpronounced vowels Listening to people talk about capsule hotels	Writing an email comparing two living spaces "The Man with No Money": Reading about living without money	"A dream come true": Finding out about a classmate's wishes **PAGE 116**
Consonant clusters Listening to descriptions of foods	Writing a recipe "Pizza: The World's Favorite Food?": Reading about the history of pizza	"Oh, really?": Surveying classmates about their experiences **PAGE 117**
Linked sounds with /w/ and /y/ Listening to travel advice	Writing an email with travel suggestions "Adventure Vacations": Reading about unusual vacations	"Fun trips": Deciding on a trip **PAGES 118, 120**
Stress in two-part verbs Listening to the results of a survey about family life	Writing a message making a request "Hotel Madness: The Crazy Things People Say!": Reading about unusual hotel requests	"I'm terribly sorry.": Apologizing and making amends **PAGE 119**
Syllable stress Listening to a radio program; listening to people give suggestions for using technology	Writing a message asking for specific favors "The Sharing Economy – Good for Everybody?": Reading about the sharing economy	"Free advice": Giving advice to classmates **PAGE 121**
Stress and rhythm Listening to a description of Carnival in Brazil	Writing an entry on a travel website about a cultural custom "Out with the Old, In with the New": Reading about interesting New Year's customs	"It's worth celebrating.": Finding out how classmates celebrate special events **PAGE 122**

Titles/Topics	Speaking	Grammar
UNIT 9 — PAGES 58–63 **Only time will tell.** Life in the past, present, and future; changes and contrasts; consequences	Talking about change; comparing time periods; describing possible consequences	Time contrasts; conditional sentences with *if* clauses
UNIT 10 — PAGES 64–69 **I like working with people.** Abilities and skills; job preferences; personality traits; careers	Describing abilities and skills; talking about job preferences; describing personality traits	Gerunds; short responses; clauses with *because*
PROGRESS CHECK — PAGES 70–71		
UNIT 11 — PAGES 72–77 **It's really worth seeing!** Landmarks and monuments; world knowledge	Talking about landmarks and monuments; describing countries; discussing facts	Passive with *by* (simple past); passive without *by* (simple present)
UNIT 12 — PAGES 78–83 **It's a long story.** Storytelling; unexpected recent past events	Describing recent past events and experiences; discussing someone's activities lately	Past continuous vs. simple past; present perfect continuous
PROGRESS CHECK — PAGES 84–85		
UNIT 13 — PAGES 86–91 **That's entertainment!** Entertainment; movies and books; reactions and opinions	Describing movies and books; talking about actors and actresses; asking for and giving reactions and opinions	Participles as adjectives; relative pronouns for people and things
UNIT 14 — PAGES 92–97 **Now I get it!** Nonverbal communication; gestures and meaning; signs; drawing conclusions	Interpreting body language; explaining gestures and meanings; describing acceptable and prohibited behavior in different situations; asking about signs and their meaning	Modals and adverbs: *might, may, could, must, maybe, perhaps, probably, definitely*; permission, obligation, and prohibition
PROGRESS CHECK — PAGES 98–99		
UNIT 15 — PAGES 100–105 **I wouldn't have done that.** Money; hopes; predicaments; speculations	Speculating about past and future events; describing a predicament; giving advice and suggestions	Unreal conditional sentences with *if* clauses; past modals
UNIT 16 — PAGES 106–111 **Making excuses** Requests; excuses; invitations	Reporting what people said; making polite requests; making invitations and excuses	Reported speech: requests and statements
PROGRESS CHECK — PAGES 112–113		
GRAMMAR PLUS — PAGES 132–150		

Pronunciation/Listening	Writing/Reading	Interchange Activity
Intonation in statements with time phrases Listening to people talk about changes	Writing a paragraph describing a person's past, present, and possible future "Aquaviva: Fighting for a Future": Reading about a town's attempt to attract new residents	"Cause and effect": Agreeing and disagreeing with classmates **PAGE 123**
Unreleased and released /t/ and /d/ Listening to people talk about their job preferences	Writing a an online cover letter for a job application "Global Work Solutions": Reading about understanding cultural differences in an international company	"You're hired.": Interviewing for a job **PAGE 124**
The letter *o* Listening to descriptions of monuments; listening for information about a country	Writing an introduction to an online city guide Reading about unusual museums	"True or false?": Sharing information about famous works **PAGE 125**
Contrastive stress in responses Listening to stories about unexpected experiences	Writing a description of a recent experience "Breaking Down the Sound of Silence": Reading about an unusual rock band	"It's my life.": Playing a board game to share past experiences **PAGE 126**
Emphatic stress Listening for opinions; listening to a movie review	Writing a movie review "The Real Art of Acting": Reading about unpleasant experiences actors put themselves through	"It was hilarious!": Asking classmates' opinions about movies, TV shows, and celebrities **PAGE 127**
Pitch Listening to people talk about the meaning of signs	Writing a list of rules "Understanding Idioms": Reading about idioms and their meaning	"Casual observers": Interpreting body language **PAGE 128**
Reduction of *have* Listening to people talk about predicaments; listening to a call-in radio show	Writing a blog post asking for advice "TOPTIPS.COM": Reading an online advice forum	"Tough choices": Deciding what to do in a difficult situation **PAGE 130**
Reduction of *had* and *would* Listening for excuses	Writing a report about people's responses to a survey "A Good Excuse for a Day Off Work": Reading about taking a sick day	"Just a bunch of excuses": Discussing calendar conflicts and making up excuses **PAGES 129, 131**

1 Good memories

▶ Ask questions to get to know people
▶ Discuss childhoods

1 SNAPSHOT

MyNeighbors

Isabel Austin
📍 Lakewood

About

🏠 **Hometown:** Chicago, Illinois, U.S.A.
💼 **Employer:** Lancaster Medical Center
🎮 **Interests:** I like to go to the movies and play video games. I also enjoy meeting people and cooking for friends.
✉ **Email:** isabelaustin@cambridge.org

MyNeighbors

Nicolás Rodriguez
📍 Lakewood

About

🏠 **Hometown:** Buenos Aires, Argentina
💼 **Employer:** Lakewood Recreation Center
🎮 **Interests:** I love skiing, swimming, camping – anything outdoors. Right now, I'm learning to skateboard.
✉ **Email:** nico_rodriguez@cup.org

Nicolás and Isabel are neighbors. Do you think they could be friends?
What social media sites do you belong to? Which one is your favorite?
Create your own online profile and share it with your classmates. What things do you have in common?

2 CONVERSATION Where did you learn to skateboard?

▶ **A** Listen and practice.

Isabel: Oh, I'm really sorry. Are you OK?
Nico: I'm fine. But I'm not very good at this.
Isabel: Neither am I . . . . Hey, I like your shirt. Are you from Argentina?
Nico: Yes, I am, originally. I was born there.
Isabel: Did you grow up there?
Nico: Yes, I did, but my family moved here 10 years ago, when I was in middle school.
Isabel: And where did you learn to skateboard?
Nico: Here in the park. I only started about a month ago.
Isabel: Well, it's my *first* time. Can you give me some lessons?
Nico: Sure. Just follow me.
Isabel: By the way, my name is Isabel.
Nico: And I'm Nico. Nice to meet you.

▶ **B** Listen to the rest of the conversation. What are two more things you learn about Isabel?

3 GRAMMAR FOCUS

▶ Past tense

Where **were** you born?
  I **was** born in Argentina.
Were you born in Buenos Aires?
  Yes, I **was**.
  No, I **wasn't**. I **was** born in Córdoba.

When **did** you **move** to Los Angeles?
  I **moved** here 10 years ago. I **didn't speak** English.
Did you **take** English classes in Argentina?
  Yes, I **did**. I **took** classes for a year.
  No, I **didn't**. My aunt **taught** me at home.

GRAMMAR PLUS *see page 132*

A Complete these conversations. Then practice with a partner.

1. **A:** Your English is very good. When _____ you begin to study English?
   B: I _____ in middle school.
   A: What _____ you think of English class at first?
   B: I _____ it was a little difficult, but fun.

2. **A:** Where _____ you born?
   B: I _____ born in Mexico.
   A: _____ you grow up there?
   B: No, I _____. I _____ up in Canada.

3. **A:** Where _____ you meet your best friend?
   B: We _____ in high school.
   A: Do you still see each other?
   B: Yes, but not very often. She _____ to South Korea two years ago.

4. **A:** _____ you have a favorite teacher when you _____ a child?
   B: Yes, I _____. I _____ a very good teacher named Mr. Potter.
   A: What _____ he teach?
   B: He _____ math.

B **PAIR WORK** Take turns asking the questions in part A. Give your own information when answering.

4 LISTENING Why did you move?

▶ **A** Listen to interviews with two immigrants to the United States. Why did they move to the U.S.A.?

▶ **B** Listen again and complete the chart.

	Enrique	Jessica
1. What were the most difficult changes?		
2. What do they miss the most?		

C **GROUP WORK** Enrique and Jessica talk about difficult changes. What could be some positive things about moving to a city like New York?

Good memories **3**

5 SPEAKING Tell me about yourself.

A **PAIR WORK** Check (✓) six questions below and add your own questions. Then interview a classmate you don't know very well. Ask follow-up questions.

- ☐ Where were your grandparents born?
- ☐ Where did they grow up?
- ☐ Did you see them a lot when you were young?
- ☐ Who's your favorite relative?
- ☐ When did you first study English?
- ☐ Can you speak other languages?
- ☐ What were your best subjects in middle school?
- ☐ What subjects didn't you like?

_____ _____

A: Where were your grandparents born?
B: My grandfather was born in Brazil, but my grandmother was born in Colombia.
A: Really? Where did they first meet?

useful expressions

Oh, that's interesting.
Really? Me, too!
Wow! Tell me more.

B **GROUP WORK** Tell the group what you learned about your partner. Then answer any questions.

"Vera's grandfather was born in Brazil, but her grandmother was born in . . ."

6 WORD POWER

A Complete the word map. Add two more words of your own to each category. Then compare with a partner.

✓ amusement park
beach
cat
collect comic books
fish
play video games
playground
stickers
teddy bear
toy cars
turtle
watch cartoons

CHILDHOOD MEMORIES

PETS

HOBBIES

PLACES
amusement park

POSSESSIONS

B **PAIR WORK** Choose three words from the word map and use them to describe some of your childhood memories.

A: I loved to watch cartoons when I was a kid.
B: Me, too. What was your favorite?
A: I liked anything with superheroes in it. What about you?

7 PERSPECTIVES When I was a kid . . .

A Listen to these statements about changes. Check (✓) those that are true about you.

☐ 1. "When I was a kid, I never used to play sports, but now I like to keep fit."
☐ 2. "I used to go out with friends a lot, but now I don't have any free time."
☐ 3. "When I was younger, I didn't use to collect anything, but now I do."
☐ 4. "I didn't use to be a good student, but now I love to study and learn new things."
☐ 5. "I never used to follow politics, but now I read the news online every morning."
☐ 6. "I used to be really neat and organized, but now I'm very messy."
☐ 7. "I used to care a lot about my appearance. Now, I'm too busy to care about how I look."

B **PAIR WORK** Look at the statements again. Which changes are positive? Which are negative?

"I think the first one is a positive change. It's good to exercise."

8 GRAMMAR FOCUS

Used to

Used to refers to something that you regularly did in the past but don't do anymore.

Did you **use to** collect things?
   Yes, I **used to** collect comic books.
   No, I **didn't use to** collect anything, but now I collect old records.

What sports **did** you **use to** play?
   I **used to play** baseball and volleyball.
   I **never used to** play sports, but now I play tennis.

GRAMMAR PLUS *see page 132*

A Complete these questions and answers. Then compare with a partner.

1. **A:** ___Did___ you ___use to___ have any pets when you were a kid?
   B: Yes, I _____ have a white cat named Snowball.
2. **A:** _____ you and your classmates _____ play together after school?
   B: No, we _____ play during the week. We _____ study a lot.
3. **A:** What music _____ you _____ listen to?
   B: I _____ listen to rock a lot. Actually, I still do.
4. **A:** What hobbies _____ you _____ have when you were little?
   B: I _____ have any hobbies, but now I play chess every week.

B How have you changed? Write sentences about yourself using *used to* or *didn't use to*. Then compare with a partner. Who has changed the most?

your hairstyle   your taste in music
your hobbies   the way you dress

> I used to wear my hair much longer.
> I didn't use to have a beard.

Good memories   **5**

9 PRONUNCIATION *Used to*

A Listen and practice. Notice that the pronunciation of *used to* and *use to* is the same.

When I was a child, I **used to** play the guitar.
I **used to** have a nickname.
I didn't **use to** like scary movies.
I didn't **use to** study very hard at school.

B **PAIR WORK** Practice the sentences you wrote in Exercise 8, part B. Pay attention to the pronunciation of *used to* and *use to*.

10 SPEAKING Memories

A **PAIR WORK** Add three questions to this list. Then take turns asking and answering the questions. Ask follow-up questions.

1. What's your favorite childhood memory?
2. What sports or games did you use to play when you were younger?
3. Did you use to have a nickname?
4. Where did you use to spend your vacations?
5. Is your taste in food different now?
6. _____
7. _____
8. _____

B **CLASS ACTIVITY** Tell the class two interesting things about your partner.

11 WRITING We used to have a lot of fun.

A Write a paragraph about things you used to do as a child. Use some of your ideas from Exercise 10.

> I grew up in a small town, and my friends and I used to play outside a lot. We used to play all kinds of games. My favorite was hide-and-seek. We also used to ride our bikes to a beautiful lake near our school...

B **GROUP WORK** Share your paragraphs and answer any questions. Did you and your classmates use to do the same things? Do kids today do the same things you used to do?

12 INTERCHANGE 1 We have a lot in common.

Find out more about your classmates. Go to Interchange 1 on page 114.

13 READING

A Scan the article. Where was Kahlo from? What happened when she was 18? Who did she marry?

A Life in Paintings: The Frida Kahlo Story

Mexican painter Frida Kahlo (1907–1954) was both a talented artist and a woman of great courage. Her paintings tell an amazing story of tragedy and hope.

At the age of six, Kahlo developed polio, and she spent nine months in bed. The illness damaged her right leg forever. Most girls didn't use to play sports back then, but Kahlo played soccer and took up boxing. Exercising helped Kahlo get stronger. Kahlo even dreamed of becoming a doctor one day.

At 18, Kahlo was in a terrible bus crash, and her destiny changed. She wore a full body cast for months because her injuries were so bad. But again, Kahlo refused to give up. She entertained herself by painting self-portraits. She said, "I paint myself because I'm often alone, and because I am the subject I know best."

Kahlo suffered from very bad health the rest of her life, but she continued to paint. Other artists began to recognize her talent – an unusual achievement for a woman at the time. In 1929, she married famous Mexican painter Diego Rivera, but their marriage was troubled. Kahlo once said, "There have been two great accidents in my life . . . Diego was by far the worst."

Kahlo became pregnant three times. Unfortunately, because of her injuries from the bus accident and her generally poor health, none of her babies survived childbirth. This sadness almost destroyed Kahlo. Her paintings often show a broken woman, both in heart and body.

When she traveled, Kahlo always attracted attention. She dressed in long traditional Mexican skirts, wore her hair in long braids, and let her thick eyebrows grow naturally. She chose to look different, and people noticed her beauty everywhere she went.

Kahlo died at the age of 47 in the house where she was born. Her life was short, but extraordinary. Her paintings still amaze people with their honesty and originality.

B Read the article. Then circle the following words in the article and match them to the definitions below.

1. courage _____
2. tragedy _____
3. destiny _____
4. cast _____
5. recognize _____
6. injury _____

a. ability to control your fear in a difficult situation
b. accept that something is good or valuable
c. damage to a person's body
d. a special hard case that protects a broken bone
e. the things that will happen in the future
f. very sad event or situation

C Answer the questions.

1. What did Kahlo do to get healthier after her childhood illness?
2. Why did Kahlo start painting?
3. Why did Kahlo often do self-portraits?
4. What did Kahlo compare her marriage to?
5. Why couldn't Kahlo have children?
6. What was unusual about Kahlo's appearance?

D **GROUP WORK** What was unusual about Kahlo's life? When do you think it's good to be different from what people expect?

Good memories 7

2 Life in the city

▸ Discuss transportation and public services
▸ Ask questions about visiting cities

1 WORD POWER Compound nouns

A Match the words in columns A and B to make compound nouns.
(More than one combination may be possible.)

subway + station = subway station

A	B
bicycle	center
bus	garage
green	jam
parking	lane
recycling	light
street	space
subway	stand
taxi	station
traffic	stop
train	system

traffic jam

green space

B **PAIR WORK** Which of these things can you find where you live?

A: There are a lot of bus lanes.   **B:** Yes. But there isn't a subway system.

2 PERSPECTIVES City services

A Listen to these opinions about city services. Match them to the correct pictures.

YOUR VOICE COUNTS!

_____ 1. The streets are dark and dangerous. I don't think there are enough police officers. And we need more streetlights.

_____ 2. There's too much pollution from cars, motorcycles, and old buses. In cities with less pollution, people are healthier.

_____ 3. There should be fewer cars, but I think that the biggest problem is parking. There just isn't enough parking.

B **PAIR WORK** Does your city or town have similar problems? What do you think is the biggest problem?

3 GRAMMAR FOCUS

▶ Expressions of quantity

With count nouns	With noncount nouns
There are **too many** cars.	There is **too much** pollution.
There should be **fewer** cars.	There should be **less** pollution.
We need **more** streetlights.	We need **more** public transportation.
There aren't **enough** police officers.	There isn't **enough** parking.

GRAMMAR PLUS see page 133

A Complete these statements about city problems. Then compare with a partner. (More than one answer may be possible.)

1. We need _____ public schools.
2. There are _____ accidents.
3. There are _____ public parks.
4. There is _____ noise all the time.
5. There is _____ recycling in our city.
6. The government should build _____ affordable housing.
7. The city needs _____ bicycle lanes.
8. There are _____ free Wi-Fi hotspots.

B **PAIR WORK** Write sentences about the city or town you are living in. Then compare with another pair.

1. The city should provide more . . .
2. We have too many . . .
3. There's too much . . .
4. There isn't enough . . .
5. There should be fewer . . .
6. We don't have enough . . .
7. There should be less . . .
8. We need more . . .

4 LISTENING It'll take forever.

▶ **A** Listen to a city resident talk to her new neighbor about the city. Check (✓) True or False for each statement.

	True	False	
1. Jacob already started his new job downtown.	☐	✓	He starts his new job tomorrow.
2. The city needs more buses.	☐	☐	
3. There aren't enough tourists in the city.	☐	☐	
4. Not many people ride bikes in the city.	☐	☐	
5. Sophia offers to lend Jacob her bike.	☐	☐	

▶ **B** Listen again. For the false statements, write the correct information.

C **PAIR WORK** What things can a city do to improve the problems that Sophia mentions? Does your city have similar problems?

Life in the city

5 DISCUSSION Rate your city.

A GROUP WORK Which of these services are available in your city or town? Discuss what is good and bad about each one.

_____ recycling system   _____ parks and green spaces   _____ affordable housing
_____ transportation system   _____ Wi-Fi service   _____ recreational and sports facilities

B GROUP WORK How would you rate the services where you live? Give each item a rating from 1 to 5.

1 = terrible   2 = needs improvement   3 = average   4 = good   5 = excellent

A: I'd give the parks a 4. There are enough parks, but they aren't always clean.
B: I think a rating of 4 is too high. There aren't enough green spaces in many areas of the city . . .

6 WRITING A social media post

A Read this post about traffic in the city on a social networking page.

B Use your statements from Exercise 3, part B, and any new ideas to write a post about a local issue.

C GROUP WORK Take turns reading your messages. Do you have any of the same concerns?

> **Posted by Michelle K**
> Today at 5:30
>
> I'm tired of this city. There's too much traffic, and it's getting worse. It used to take me 15 minutes to get to class. Today it took me more than 30 minutes during rush hour! There should be more subway lines. I think people want to use public transportation, but we need more . . .
>
> comment

7 SNAPSHOT

Common Tourist Questions

- [ ] What's the best way to see the city?
- [ ] How much do taxis cost?
- [ ] Which hotel is closest to the airport?
- [ ] Where should I go shopping?
- [ ] What festivals or events are taking place?
- [ ] Where can I buy a SIM card for my phone?
- [ ] Where's a good place to meet friends?
- [ ] Where can I get a city guide?
- [ ] What museums should I see?
- [ ] What are some family-friendly activities?

Check (✓) the questions you can answer about your city.
What other questions could a visitor ask about your city?
Talk to your classmates. Find answers to the questions you didn't check.

8 CONVERSATION Do you know where . . . ?

A Listen and practice.

Rachel: Excuse me. Do you know where the nearest ATM is?
Clerk: There's one down the street, across from the café.
Rachel: Great. And do you know where I can catch a bus downtown?
Clerk: Sure. Just look for the signs for "Public Transportation."
Rachel: OK. And can you tell me how often they run?
Clerk: They run every 10 minutes or so.
Rachel: And just one more thing. Could you tell me where the restrooms are?
Clerk: Right inside. Do you see where that sign is?
Rachel: Oh. Thanks a lot.

B Listen to the rest of the conversation. Check (✓) the information that Rachel asks for.

☐ the cost of the bus fare ☐ the location of a taxi stand
☐ the cost of a city guide ☐ the location of a bookstore

9 GRAMMAR FOCUS

Indirect questions from Wh-questions

Wh-questions with *be*	Indirect questions
Where is the nearest ATM?	Could you tell me **where the nearest ATM is**?
Where are the restrooms?	Do you know **where the restrooms are**?

Wh-questions with *do*	Indirect questions
How often do the buses run?	Can you tell me **how often the buses run**?
What time does the bookstore open?	Do you know **what time the bookstore opens**?

Wh-questions with *can*	Indirect questions
Where can I catch the bus?	Do you know **where I can catch the bus**?

GRAMMAR PLUS see page 133

A Write indirect questions using these Wh-questions. Then compare with a partner.

1. Where can I rent a car?
2. How much does a city tour cost?
3. How early do the stores open?
4. Where's the nearest Wi-Fi hotspot?
5. How much does a taxi to the airport cost?
6. What time does the post office open?
7. Where's an inexpensive hotel in this area?
8. How late do the nightclubs stay open?

B PAIR WORK Take turns asking and answering the questions you wrote in part A.

A: Do you know where I can rent a car?
B: You can rent one at the airport.

Life in the city 11

10 PRONUNCIATION Syllable stress

A Listen and practice. Notice which syllable has the main stress in these two-syllable words.

● ·   · ●
subway   garage
traffic   police

B Listen to the stress in these words. Write them in the correct columns. Then compare with a partner.

	● ·	· ●
buses improve	_____	_____
bookstore provide	_____	_____
event public	_____	_____
hotel taxis	_____	_____

11 SPEAKING The best of our town

A Complete the chart with indirect questions.

	Name:
1. Where's the best area to stay? "Do you know where the best area to stay is?"	
2. What's the best way to see the city? "_____?"	
3. How late do the buses run? "_____?"	
4. How much do people tip in a restaurant? "_____?"	
5. What's a good restaurant to try the local food? "_____?"	
6. What are the most popular attractions? "_____?"	
7. Where can I hear live music? "_____?"	

B **PAIR WORK** Use the indirect questions in the chart to interview a classmate about the city or town where you live. Take notes.

A: Do you know where the best area to stay is?
B: It depends. You can stay near . . .

C **CLASS ACTIVITY** Share your answers with the class. Who knows the most about your city or town?

12 INTERCHANGE 2 Top travel destinations

Discuss ways to attract tourists to a city. Go to Interchange 2 on page 115.

13 READING

A Skim the article. Which of the following things does it mention?

transportation   natural areas   safety   entertainment   schools   housing

The World's Happiest Cities 😊

Home   About   Articles   Community   Traveling   Food   Booking

When author Dan Buettner went looking for the world's happiest people on four different continents, he found some really great places to live!

___ **a.** Singapore
With a population of 5.1 million, Singapore is really crowded, and people work very long hours. Yet 95 percent of Singapore residents say they are happy. Subway trains almost always arrive on time. The police are good at their jobs and always ready to help. People in Singapore love that their city is so clean and safe.

___ **b.** Aarhus, Denmark
Although people pay an incredible 68 percent of their salaries in taxes here, they get lots of services for free: healthcare, education, and daycare for young children. The city has lots of entertainment options too, like museums, shopping, and nightlife. For those who love nature, it's only a 15-minute bike ride to incredible beaches and forests.

___ **c.** San Luis Obispo, California, U.S.A.
People here smile and feel happy more than in any other American city. Most people travel less than 10 minutes to work, and there are lots of bike lanes, so commuting is easy. Residents share their joy with others, too. Almost 25 percent of people in San Luis Obispo volunteer to help people in their free time.

___ **d.** Monterrey, Mexico
Although many of its people don't earn high salaries, they still feel rich. People in Monterrey have strong family relationships and very busy social lives. They also have a positive attitude about life – they laugh and stay strong even in times of trouble.

Adapted from http://www.rd.com/advice/travel/the-4-happiest-cities-on-earth

B Read the article. Match the paragraphs (a–d) to the pictures (1–4).

C Read the comments from residents of these four cities. Which city do you think they live in? Write the letter.

1. "I spend a lot of time with my relatives." ___
2. "A lot of what I earn goes to the government, but I don't mind." ___
3. "I can see great art in my city." ___
4. "I often have to spend eleven hours or more in the office." ___
5. "I help children with their homework after school for free." ___
6. "I try to be cheerful, even when things are going badly." ___
7. "I take the train to work, and I'm never late." ___
8. "On weekends, I can get out of the city without taking the car." ___

D PAIR WORK Which sentences in part C are true for you and your city or town? How would you improve the place where you live?

Life in the city

Units 1–2 Progress check

SELF-ASSESSMENT

How well can you do these things? Check (✓) the boxes.

I can . . .	Very well	OK	A little
Understand descriptions of childhood (Ex. 1)	☐	☐	☐
Ask and answer questions about childhood and past times (Ex. 1, 2)	☐	☐	☐
Express opinions about cities and towns; agree and disagree (Ex. 3)	☐	☐	☐
Ask for and give information about a city or town (Ex. 4)	☐	☐	☐

1 LISTENING What was that like?

A Listen to an interview with Charlotte, a fashion designer. Answer the questions in complete sentences.

1. Where did she grow up? What is her hometown like?
2. What did she want to do when she grew up?
3. What were her hobbies as a child?
4. What sport did she use to play?
5. What was her favorite place? What did she use to do there?

B PAIR WORK Use the questions in part A to interview a partner about his or her childhood. Ask follow-up questions to get more information.

2 DISCUSSION In the past, . . .

A PAIR WORK Talk about how life in your country has changed in the last 50 years. Ask questions like these:

What kinds of homes did people live in?
How did people use to communicate?
What did people use to do in their free time?
How did people use to dress?
How were schools different?
What kinds of jobs did men have? women?

A: What kinds of homes did people live in?
B: Houses used to be bigger. Now most people live in small apartments.

B GROUP WORK Compare your answers. Do you think life was better in the past? Why or why not?

3 SURVEY Are there enough parks?

A What do you think about these things in your city or town? Complete the survey.

	Not enough	OK	Too many/Too much
free shows and concerts	☐	☐	☐
places to go dancing	☐	☐	☐
parks and green spaces	☐	☐	☐
places to go shopping	☐	☐	☐
noise	☐	☐	☐
places to sit and have coffee	☐	☐	☐
public transportation	☐	☐	☐
places to meet new people	☐	☐	☐

B **GROUP WORK** Compare your opinions and suggest ways to make your city or town better. Then agree on three improvements.

A: How would you make our city better?
B: There should be more shows and concerts. There aren't enough free activities for young people.
C: I disagree. There should be more schools. We don't need more entertainment.

4 ROLE PLAY Can I help you?

Student A: Imagine you are a visitor in your city or town. Write five indirect questions about these categories. Then ask your questions to the hotel front-desk clerk.

Transportation   Sightseeing
Hotels   Shopping
Restaurants   Entertainment

Student B: You are a hotel front-desk clerk. Answer the guest's questions.

A: Excuse me.
B: Can I help you?

Change roles and try the role play again.

useful expressions

Let me think. Oh, yes, . . .
I'm not really sure, but I think . . .
Sorry, I don't know.

WHAT'S NEXT?

Look at your Self-assessment again. Do you need to review anything?

3 Making changes

▶ Compare houses and apartments
▶ Discuss life changes

1 WORD POWER Homes

A These words are used to describe houses and apartments. Which are positive (**P**)? Which are negative (**N**)?

bright	____	dingy	____	private	____
comfortable	____	expensive	____	quiet	____
convenient	____	huge	____	run-down	____
cramped	____	inconvenient	____	safe	____
dangerous	____	modern	____	small	____
dark	____	noisy	____	spacious	____

cramped

B **PAIR WORK** Tell your partner two positive and two negative features of your house or apartment.

"I live in a nice neighborhood. It's safe and very convenient. However, the apartment is a little cramped and kind of expensive."

2 PERSPECTIVES How's your new apartment?

A Listen to a family talk about their new apartment. Which opinions are about the building or the neighborhood? Which are about the apartment?

1. I don't like living in an apartment. We don't have as much privacy as we had in our old place.
2. I just can't sleep at night. The neighbors make too much noise. The building isn't as quiet as our old one.
3. The new apartment is too dark and too hot. There aren't enough windows.
4. Our new apartment isn't big enough for our family. We don't have a big kitchen anymore, so cooking is difficult.
5. The location is just as convenient as the old one, but there aren't as many good restaurants around.

B **PAIR WORK** Look at the opinions again. Talk about similar problems you have.

A: My next-door neighbors make too much noise. They have parties every Saturday.
B: My brother has the same problem. His neighbor's band practices all weekend!

3 GRAMMAR FOCUS

▶ Evaluations and comparisons

Evaluations with adjectives
Our apartment is**n't** big **enough** for our family.
This apartment is **too** hot.

Comparisons with adjectives
The building is**n't as** quiet **as** our old one.
The location is **just as** convenient **as** the old one.

Evaluations with nouns
There are**n't enough** windows.
The neighbors make **too much** noise.

Comparisons with nouns
We do**n't** have **as many** bedrooms **as** we used to.
We do**n't** have **as much** privacy **as** we had.

GRAMMAR PLUS see page 134

A Imagine you are looking for a house or an apartment to rent. Read the two ads. Then rewrite the opinions using the words in parentheses. Compare with a partner.

For rent
Spacious, modern house
3 bedrooms, 1 bathroom; in quiet suburb 20 miles from downtown; 2-car garage; $1500 per month.

For rent
Comfortable apartment
2 bedrooms, 1 bathroom; downtown, near subway; 1 parking space; built in 1920; $900 per month.

1. The house is 20 miles from downtown. (too)
2. It's not convenient enough. (too)
3. It has only one bathroom. (not enough)
4. The rent is very high. (too)
5. The apartment is too old. (not enough)
6. There are only two bedrooms. (not enough)
7. It's not spacious enough. (too)
8. There's only one parking space. (not enough)

It's too far from downtown.

B Write comparisons of the house and the apartment using these words and *as . . . as*. Then compare with a partner.

big	noisy
bedrooms	expensive
bathrooms	modern
spacious	convenient
private	parking spaces

The apartment isn't as big as the house.
The apartment doesn't have as many bedrooms as the house.

C **GROUP WORK** Which would you prefer to rent: the house or the apartment? Why?

A: I'd choose the apartment. The house isn't close enough to public transportation.
B: I'd rent the house because the apartment is too small.

Making changes

4 PRONUNCIATION Unpronounced vowels

A Listen and practice. The vowel immediately after a stressed syllable is sometimes not pronounced.

av̶e̶rage   comf̶o̶rtable
diff̶e̶rent   int̶e̶resting
sep̶a̶rate   veg̶e̶table

B Write four sentences using some of the words in part A. Then read them with a partner. Pay attention to unpronounced vowels.

Today, the average house is much smaller than 50 years ago.

5 LISTENING A home away from home

A Listen to Josh describe a "capsule hotel." Check (✓) True or False for each statement.

	True	False	
1. Tokyo sometimes feels too noisy.	☐	✓	Sometimes it feels too big.
2. A capsule hotel is not as convenient as a regular hotel.	☐	☐	
3. Inside every capsule there is a TV, a radio, and an alarm clock.	☐	☐	
4. The capsule is a good option if you're busy and tired.	☐	☐	
5. Josh would recommend a capsule hotel to anyone.	☐	☐	

B Listen again. For the false statements, write the correct information.

C GROUP WORK Where else do you think a capsule hotel would be popular? Why?

6 WRITING My new home

A Imagine you've just moved to this apartment. Write an email to a friend comparing your old home to your new one.

Hi Chloe,
How's everything? I have some great news. We just moved to a new apartment! Do you remember our old apartment? It was too small, and I didn't have enough space for my things. My new bedroom is spacious, and I have a separate area to study in. The apartment also has a balcony. It isn't very big, but now we can have breakfast outdoors on Sundays. The . . .

B PAIR WORK Read each other's emails. How are your descriptions similar? different?

7 SNAPSHOT

MAKE A WISH

- ☐ Have a healthier lifestyle
- ☐ Start my own business
- ☐ Enjoy life more
- ☐ Add more hours to the day
- ☐ Do volunteer work
- ☐ Go back to school
- ☐ Improve my personality
- ☐ Move to a new home
- ☐ Make new friends
- ☐ Spend more time with my family

Check (✓) some of the things you would like to do. Then tell a partner why.
Which of these wishes would be easy to achieve? Which would be difficult or impossible?
What other things would you like to change about your life? Why?

8 CONVERSATION I wish I could.

A Listen and practice.

Harry: So, are you still living with your parents, Dylan?
Dylan: Yes, I am. But sometimes I wish I had my own apartment.
Harry: Why? Don't you like living at home?
Dylan: It's OK, but my parents are always asking me to come home early. I wish they'd stop worrying about me.
Harry: Yeah, parents are like that!
Dylan: Plus, they don't like my friends, and they won't stop criticizing them. I wish life weren't so difficult.
Harry: So, why don't you move out?
Dylan: Hey, I wish I could, but where else can I get free room and board?

B Listen to the rest of the conversation. What changes would Harry like to make in his life?

Making changes

9 GRAMMAR FOCUS

Wish

Use wish + past tense to refer to present wishes.

I **live** with my parents.
   I wish I **didn't live** with my parents.
   I wish I **had** my own apartment.
I **can't move** out.
   I wish I **could move** out.

Life **is** difficult.
   I wish it **were*** easier.
   I wish it **weren't** so difficult.
My parents **won't stop** worrying about me.
   I wish they **would stop** worrying about me.

*For the verb *be*, *were* is used with all pronouns after *wish*.

GRAMMAR PLUS see page 134

A Read these other comments that Dylan makes. Then rewrite the sentences using *wish*. (More than one answer is possible.)

1. My mother doesn't like my girlfriend.   <u>I wish she liked my girlfriend.</u>
2. My girlfriend is too short to be a model.   <u>She wishes she were taller.</u>
3. My classes are really boring.
4. I'm not on vacation right now.
5. My family can't afford a bigger house.
6. The neighbors won't stop making noise.
7. Harry doesn't like his job.

B **PAIR WORK** Think of five things you wish you could change. Then discuss them with your partner.

A: What do you wish you could change?
B: Well, I don't have much free time. I wish I had time to . . .

10 SPEAKING Make it happen.

A If you could wish for three things, what would they be? Write down your wishes.

B **GROUP WORK** How can you make your wishes come true? Get suggestions from your classmates.

A: I wish I had more money.
B: Why don't you look for another job?
A: I don't have enough experience. I wish I had a diploma.
C: You can go back to school or take an online course.

11 INTERCHANGE 3 A dream come true

Find out more about your classmates' wishes. Go to Interchange 3 on page 116.

12 READING

A Skim the article. Which of these sentences is true?

Boyle decided that a life without money was impossible to live.

Boyle wanted to give people the chance to live a different lifestyle.

THE MAN WITH NO MONEY

A Can you imagine your life without any money? Not even a cent, a real, or a peso? One man decided to try it out.

B Mark Boyle was a successful manager of an organic food company in Ireland. He had a good life. But he worried about the damage humans were doing to the environment. He also believed people bought more things than they needed. Boyle wished we grew our own food and made our own furniture, so we wouldn't waste as much as we do today. So one day, he left his job and started an experiment – could he live for a year without buying anything?

C He sold his houseboat and moved into an old mobile home. He got it for free from a website where people give away things they don't want. It wasn't as comfortable as his old place at first, but he soon made it feel like home. He parked it on a farm near Bristol, England. Instead of paying rent, he worked on the farm. He burned wood from the forest to heat his home, so he didn't pay electricity or gas bills.

D Boyle didn't go shopping, either. He grew his own fruit and vegetables. He also looked for food in the trash cans of supermarkets and cooked it on a wood stove. He made his own toothpaste from fish bones and seeds. To wash his clothes, he used a special type of nut to make soap. Boyle even built his own toilet and used old newspapers from the farm for toilet paper.

E He began using money again after eighteen months. He says his life change made him feel healthier, happier, and closer to nature. He wrote two books about his experience and used the money to start "The Free House," a farm in Ireland where people can live without money.

B Read the article. Then circle the correct word or words.

1. Before the experiment, Mark Boyle was **good at / unhappy with** his job.
2. Boyle thought that people **spent too much / discussed money too often**.
3. Boyle worked on a farm **to earn money to pay rent / so he didn't have to pay rent**.
4. Boyle made cleaning products from things he found in **trash cans / the forest**.
5. Boyle generally felt **worse / better** after living without money.

C Match the sentences to the paragraphs they describe. Write the letter.

_____ 1. Describes a big change that happened in the person's life
_____ 2. Describes the way the person's everyday habits changed
_____ 3. Asks a question to make the reader think about the topic
_____ 4. Gives general information about the past of the main person in the story
_____ 5. Explains how the person felt about the whole experiment

D **PAIR WORK** Discuss Boyle's experience. Would you like to try it?

Do you think people today spend too much money on things they don't need?

Making changes

4 Have you ever tried it?

▸ Describe past personal experiences
▸ Discuss food, recipes, and cooking methods

1 SNAPSHOT

TRADITIONAL DISHES FROM AROUND THE WORLD

Lebanon	South Korea	Singapore	Brazil
Kibbeh Labanieh	Galbi	Gulai Kepala Ikan	Moqueca
Lamb or beef meatballs cooked in yogurt with spices	Korean-style barbecued meat	A dish made from a fish head cooked in a rich curry sauce	Fish and shellfish stew cooked in coconut milk in a clay pot

Which dishes are made with meat? with fish?
Have you ever tried any of these dishes? Which ones would you like to try?
What traditional foods are popular in your country?

2 CONVERSATION I've never heard of that!

A Listen and practice.

Aiden: Hey, this sounds strange – frog legs with butter and garlic sauce. Have you ever eaten frog legs?

Claire: Yes, I have. I had them here just last week.

Aiden: Did you like them?

Claire: Yes, I did. They were delicious! Why don't you try some?

Aiden: No, I don't think so. I'm a little scared of them.

Server: Have you decided on an appetizer yet?

Claire: Yes. I'll have a small order of frog legs, please.

Server: And you, sir?

Aiden: I think I'll have the snails.

Claire: Snails? That's adventurous of you!

B Listen to the rest of the conversation. How did Aiden like the snails? What else did he order?

3 PRONUNCIATION Consonant clusters

A Listen and practice. Notice how the two consonants at the beginning of a word are pronounced together.

/k/	/t/	/m/	/n/	/p/	/r/	/l/
scan	start	smart	snack	spare	brown	blue
skim	step	smile	snow	speak	gray	play

B **PAIR WORK** Find one more word on page 22 for each consonant cluster in part A. Then practice saying the words.

4 GRAMMAR FOCUS

Simple past vs. present perfect

Use the simple past for experiences at a definite time in the past.
Use the present perfect for experiences within a time period up to the present.

Have you ever **eaten** frog legs?
   Yes, I **have**. I **tried** them last month.
Did you **like** them?
   Yes, I **did**. They **were** delicious.

Have you ever **been** to a Vietnamese restaurant?
   No, I **haven't**. But I **ate** at a Thai restaurant last night.
Did you **go** alone?
   No, I **went** with some friends.

GRAMMAR PLUS see page 135

A Complete these conversations. Then practice with a partner.

1. **A:** Have you ever _____eaten_____ (eat) sushi?
   B: Yes, I _____. In fact, I _____ (eat) some just last week.

2. **A:** Have you ever _____ (try) Moroccan food?
   B: No, I _____, but I'd like to.

3. **A:** Did you _____ (have) breakfast today?
   B: Yes, I _____. I _____ (eat) a huge breakfast.

4. **A:** Have you ever _____ (be) to a picnic at the beach?
   B: Yes, I _____. My family and I _____ (have) a picnic on the beach last month. We _____ (cook) hamburgers.

5. **A:** Did you _____ (cook) dinner last night?
   B: Yes, I _____. I _____ (make) spaghetti with tomato sauce.

B **PAIR WORK** Ask and answer the questions in part A. Give your own information.

5 LISTENING Have you tried this before?

A Listen to six people ask questions in a restaurant. Are they talking about these items? Write **Y** (yes) or **N** (no).

1. _N_ plate
   juice
2. ___ the check
   _____
3. ___ cake
   _____
4. ___ meat
   _____
5. ___ water
   _____
6. ___ the menu
   _____

B Listen again. For the no (**N**) items, write what they might be talking about instead.

Have you ever tried it? **23**

6 SPEAKING How did you like it?

PAIR WORK Ask your partner these questions and four more of your own. Then ask follow-up questions.

Have you ever drunk fresh sugar cane juice?
Have you ever been to a vegetarian restaurant?
Have you ever had an unusual ice cream flavor?
Have you ever eaten something you didn't like?

A: Have you ever drunk fresh sugar cane juice?
B: Yes, I have. I drank it in Egypt once.
A: How did you like it?
B: I loved it, actually.

7 INTERCHANGE 4 Oh, really?

Find out some interesting facts about your classmates. Go to Interchange 4 on page 117.

8 WORD POWER Cooking methods

A How do you cook the foods below? Check (✓) the methods that are most common.

bake   boil   fry   grill   roast   steam

Methods	Foods								
	fish	shrimp	eggs	chicken	beef	potatoes	onions	corn	bananas
bake	☐	☐	☐	☐	☐	☐	☐	☐	☐
boil	☐	☐	☐	☐	☐	☐	☐	☐	☐
fry	☐	☐	☐	☐	☐	☐	☐	☐	☐
grill	☐	☐	☐	☐	☐	☐	☐	☐	☐
roast	☐	☐	☐	☐	☐	☐	☐	☐	☐
steam	☐	☐	☐	☐	☐	☐	☐	☐	☐

B **PAIR WORK** What's your favorite way to cook or eat the foods in part A?

A: Have you ever fried bananas?
B: No, I haven't. But sometimes I grill them.

9 PERSPECTIVES Comfort food

A Listen to this recipe for macaroni and cheese. Do you think this is a healthy dish?

Baked Macaroni and Cheese

- 1 package elbow macaroni
- 4 tablespoons butter
- 2 cups heavy cream
- 4 cups cheddar cheese, shredded

First, boil the macaroni in a large pot for 5 minutes. Then melt the butter on medium heat and add the cream. Stir for about 2 minutes. Next, add the cheese. Stir until the cheese is melted. Season with salt and pepper. After that, add the cooked macaroni and mix well. Finally, bake for 20 minutes.

B **PAIR WORK** Look at the steps in the recipe again. Number the pictures from 1 to 5. Would you like to try this traditional American dish?

10 GRAMMAR FOCUS

Sequence adverbs

First, boil the macaroni in a large pot.
Then melt the butter on medium heat.
Next, add the cheese.
After that, add the cooked macaroni.
Finally, bake for 20 minutes.

GRAMMAR PLUS see page 135

A Here's a recipe for a couscous salad. Look at the pictures and number the steps from 1 to 5. Then add a sequence adverb to each step.

- ☐ _____ drain the couscous and let it cool.
- ☐ 1 _First,_____ chop some olives, parsley, and cheese.
- ☐ _____ toss the cooked couscous with the olives, parsley, and cheese.
- ☐ _____ pour some couscous into the hot water and let it sit for 10 minutes.
- ☐ _____ boil a pot of water.

B **PAIR WORK** Cover the recipe and look only at the pictures. Explain each step of the recipe to your partner.

Have you ever tried it?

11 LISTENING How do you make it?

A Listen to people explain how to make these snacks. Which snack are they talking about? Number the photos from 1 to 4. (There is one extra photo.)

| spaghetti | chocolate chip cookies | salsa | French toast | popcorn |

B Listen again. Check (✓) the steps you hear for each recipe.

1. ✓ add
   ✓ chop
   ☐ heat

2. ☐ cut
   ☐ heat
   ☐ pour

3. ☐ stir
   ☐ cook
   ☐ cover

4. ☐ mix
   ☐ bake
   ☐ mash

C PAIR WORK Tell your partner how to make one of the snacks above. Your partner will guess which snack it is.

12 SPEAKING It's my favorite food.

GROUP WORK Discuss these questions.

What's your favorite food?
Is it easy to make?
What's in it?
How often do you eat it?
Where do you usually eat it?
How healthy is it?

"My favorite food is pizza. It's not difficult to make. First, . . ."

13 WRITING My cookbook

A Read this recipe. Is this an easy recipe to make?

Guacamole

First, chop the tomato, onion, chili pepper, and cilantro. Then scoop out the flesh of the avocados and mash it with a fork. Next, squeeze the lime and mix the juice with the avocado. Finally, combine all the ingredients, mix well, and season with salt to taste.

1 tomato
half a red onion
3 avocados
1 lime
1 fresh green chili pepper
2 tablespoons cilantro

B Now think of something you know how to make. First, write down the things you need. Then describe how to make it.

C GROUP WORK Read and discuss each recipe. Then choose one to share with the class. Explain why you chose it.

Unit 4

14 READING

A Scan the article. Which city does pizza come from? When did pizza arrive in New York? What do people in Japan like on their pizzas?

PIZZA:
The World's Favorite Food?

Food, and the way we eat it, is always changing. As society develops, we learn new ways of growing, processing, and cooking food. [a] Also, when people travel to live in other countries, they take their knowledge of cooking with them. And food must fit modern lifestyles and local tastes, too. One food that has done this successfully is the pizza.

The pizza we recognize today first appeared in Italy in 1889. A famous baker from Naples made a special pizza for the Italian royal family. [b] Queen Margherita loved the dish so much, the baker named it after her. Since then, this simple meal of bread, cheese, and tomato has traveled the world, and it has adapted to local cultures.

Pizza began its journey in the 1890s, when many Italians moved to New York in search of a better life. There they continued to make pizzas, and the first pizzeria opened in 1905.

At first it was only popular with Italians, but by the late 1940s, Americans discovered a taste for it. Today, they spend an incredible $37 billion a year on pizzas. [c]

Pizza continued its travels around the world, adapting all the time. In Sweden, for example, it is not unusual to have peanuts and bananas on your pizza. [d] Japan is a nation of seafood lovers, so not surprisingly, they love octopus and squid, as well as roasted seaweed, toppings. Australians sometimes choose kangaroo or crocodile, and in the Philippines they like mango on their pizza.

The popularity of the pizza is also related to our changing lifestyles. In today's super-fast society, people often don't have the time or energy to cook. So, they order takeout – and very often, it's a pizza. [e] If you don't even have time to sit down, buy a single slice and eat it standing up!

The pizza has come a long way. From its beginnings in an Italian city, it has grown to become one of the world's favorite foods.

B Read the article. Where do these sentences belong? Write the letters a–e.

___ 1. That's more than $100 per American!
___ 2. What we ate 200 years ago was very different from what we eat today.
___ 3. In Belgium, people eat chocolate pizzas with marshmallows on top.
___ 4. Sometimes you don't even have to pick it up; it's delivered to your home.
___ 5. He was very worried they wouldn't like it, but they did.

C How has local food changed in your country in the last 50 years? What new foods do you eat now that you didn't eat before?

Have you ever tried it?

Units 3–4 Progress check

SELF-ASSESSMENT

How well can you do these things? Check (✓) the boxes.

I can . . .	Very well	OK	A little
Evaluate a house or apartment (Ex. 1)	☐	☐	☐
Express opinions about houses or apartments; agree and disagree (Ex. 1)	☐	☐	☐
Discuss life changes (Ex. 2)	☐	☐	☐
Describe past personal experiences (Ex. 3)	☐	☐	☐
Describe recipes (Ex. 4)	☐	☐	☐

1 SPEAKING For rent

A PAIR WORK Use the topics in the box to write an ad for an apartment. Use this ad as a model. Make the apartment sound as good as possible.

FOR RENT

Comfortable 1-bedroom apartment

Spacious, bright; located downtown; convenient to public transportation; 1 bathroom, modern kitchen; 1-car garage

$1200 a month

---

age	windows	parking
size	bathroom(s)	cost
location	bedroom(s)	noise

B GROUP WORK Join another pair. Evaluate and compare the apartments. Which would you prefer to rent? Why?

A: There aren't enough bedrooms in your apartment.
B: But it's convenient.
C: Yes, but our apartment is just as convenient!

2 LISTENING Making changes

▶ A Listen to three people talk about things they wish they could change. Check (✓) the topic each person is talking about.

1. ☐ city   ☐ travel   _____
2. ☐ school ☐ skills   _____
3. ☐ free time ☐ money _____

▶ B Listen again. Write one change each person would like to make.

C PAIR WORK Use the topics in part A to express your own wishes.

3 SURVEY Memorable meals

A Complete the survey with your food opinions and experiences. Then use your information to write questions.

Me	Name
1. I've eaten _____. I liked it. _Have you ever eaten_ ? _Did you like it_ ?	
2. I've eaten _____. I hated it. _____ ? _____ ?	
3. I've never tried _____. But I want to. _____ ?	
4. I've been to the restaurant _____ I enjoyed it. _____ ?	
5. I've made _____ for my friends. They loved it. _____ ?	

B **CLASS ACTIVITY** Go around the class and ask your questions. Find people who have had the same experiences as you. Write a classmate's name only once.

A: Have you ever eaten a sloppy joe sandwich?
B: Yes, I have.
A: Did you like it?
B: Yes . . . but it was too messy.

4 ROLE PLAY Reality cooking competition

GROUP WORK Work in groups of four. Two students are the judges. Two students are the chefs.

Judges: Make a list of three ingredients for the chefs to use. You will decide which chef creates the best recipe.

Chefs: Think of a recipe using the three ingredients the judges give you and other basic ingredients. Name the recipe and describe how to make it. "My recipe is called . . . . To make it, first . . . . Then . . . . Next, ..."

Change roles and try the role play again.

WHAT'S NEXT?

Look at your Self-assessment again. Do you need to review anything?

Units 3–4 Progress check

5 Hit the road!

▶ Discuss vacation and travel plans
▶ Give travel advice

1 SNAPSHOT

What do you like to do on vacation?

take a fun trip | discover something new | stay home | enjoy nature

- ☐ visit a foreign country
- ☐ travel in my own country
- ☐ go to a music festival
- ☐ take a photography course
- ☐ hang out with friends
- ☐ host a family reunion
- ☐ go camping
- ☐ relax at the beach

Which activities do you like to do on vacation? Check (✓) the activities.
Which activities would you like to do on your next vacation?
Make a list of other activities you like to do on vacation. Then compare with a partner.

2 CONVERSATION I guess I'll just stay home.

A Listen and practice.

Nora: I'm so excited! We have two weeks off! What are you going to do?
Lily: I'm not sure. I guess I'll just stay home. Maybe I'll hang out with some friends and watch my favorite series. What about you? Any plans?
Nora: Yeah, I'm going to relax at the beach with my cousin. We're going to go surfing every day. And my cousin likes to snorkel, so maybe we'll go snorkeling one day.
Lily: Sounds like fun.
Nora: Hey, why don't you come with us?
Lily: Do you mean it? I'd love to! I'll bring my surfboard!
Nora: That's great! The more the merrier!

B Listen to the rest of the conversation. Where are they going to stay? How will they get there?

3 GRAMMAR FOCUS

▶ Future with *be going to* and *will*

Use *be going to* + verb for plans you've decided on.

What **are** you **going to do**?
 I'm going to relax at the beach.
 We're **going to go** surfing every day.
 I'm not **going to do** anything special.

Use *will* + verb for possible plans before you've made a decision.

What **are** you **going to do**?
 I'm not sure. I **guess I'll** just **stay** home.
 Maybe I'll take a course.
 I don't know. I **think I'll go** camping.
 I **probably won't go** anywhere.

GRAMMAR PLUS see page 136

A Complete the conversation with appropriate forms of *be going to* or *will*. Then compare with a partner.

1. **A:** Have you made any vacation plans?
   B: Well, I've decided on one thing – I _____ take a bike tour.
   A: That's great! For how long?
   B: I _____ be away for about a week. I need to take some time off.
   A: So, when are you leaving?
   B: I'm not sure. I _____ probably leave around the end of next month.
   A: And where _____ you _____ go?
   B: I haven't thought about that yet. I guess I _____ go down south.
   A: That sounds like fun. _____ you _____ buy a new bicycle?
   B: I'm not sure. Actually, I probably _____ buy one – I don't have enough money right now. I guess I _____ rent one.
   A: _____ you _____ go with anyone?
   B: No. I need some time alone. I _____ travel by myself.

2. **A:** What are your plans for the holiday weekend?
   B: I _____ visit my parents.
   A: What _____ you _____ do there?
   B: Nothing much. I _____ hang out with some old school friends. And we _____ probably have a barbecue on Sunday.
   A: That sounds like fun. When _____ you _____ leave?
   B: I'm not sure yet. I _____ probably leave on Friday night if I don't need to work on Saturday.
   A: _____ you _____ fly there?
   B: I wish I could, but it's too expensive. I guess I _____ take the train.
   A: _____ you _____ go alone?
   B: Maybe my brother _____ go, too. He hasn't decided yet.
   A: Do you know when you are coming back?
   B: I think I _____ come back on Monday.
   A: Good. Then we can have dinner together on Monday.

B Have you thought about your next vacation? Write answers to these questions. (If you already have plans, use *be going to*. If you don't have fixed plans, use *will*.)

1. How are you going to spend your next vacation?
2. Where are you going to go?
3. When are you going to take your vacation?
4. How long are you going to be on vacation?
5. Is anyone going to travel with you?

> I'm going to spend my next vacation . . .
> OR I'm not sure. Maybe I'll . . .

C GROUP WORK Take turns telling the group about your vacation plans. Use your information from part B.

Hit the road! **31**

4 WORD POWER Travel preparations

A Complete the chart. Then add one more word to each category.

ATM card	cash	medication	plane ticket	swimsuit
backpack	first-aid kit	money belt	sandals	travel insurance
carry-on bag	hiking boots	passport	suitcase	vaccination

Clothing	Money	Health	Documents	Luggage

B **PAIR WORK** What are the five most important items you need for these vacations?

a beach vacation   a rafting trip   a trip to a foreign country

5 INTERCHANGE 5 Fun trips

Decide between two vacations. Student A, go to Interchange 5A on page 118; Student B, go to Interchange 5B on page 120.

6 PERSPECTIVES Travel advisor

A Listen to these pieces of advice from experienced travelers. What topic is each person talking about?

"You must have a valid passport to travel overseas. You ought to make a copy of your passport and keep it in a secure place."

"When you fly, you should keep important things in your carry-on bag, such as your medication and ATM card. You shouldn't pack them in your checked luggage."

"You should try some of the local specialties, but you'd better avoid the stalls on the street. You shouldn't drink tap water."

"In most countries, you don't have to have an international driver's license, but you have to carry a license from your own country. You also need to be 21 or over."

"You'd better buy travel insurance before you leave your country."

"You'd better keep a copy of your credit card numbers at the hotel. And you shouldn't carry a lot of cash when you go out."

B **PAIR WORK** Look at the advice again. Do you think this is all good advice? Why or why not?

7 GRAMMAR FOCUS

Modals for necessity and suggestion

Describing necessity	Giving suggestions
You **must** have health insurance.	You**'d better** avoid the stalls on the street.
You **need to** be 21 or over.	You **ought to** make a copy of your passport.
You **have to** get a passport.	You **should** try some local specialties.
You **don't have to** get vaccinations.	You **shouldn't** carry a lot of cash.

GRAMMAR PLUS see page 136

A Choose the best advice for someone who is going on vacation. Then compare with a partner.

1. You _____ pack too many clothes. You won't have room to bring back any gifts. (don't have to / shouldn't)
2. You _____ carry identification with you. It's the law! (must / should)
3. You _____ buy a money belt to carry your passport, ATM card, and cash. (have to / ought to)
4. You _____ make hotel reservations in advance. It might be difficult to find a room after you get there. (have to / 'd better)
5. You _____ buy a round-trip plane ticket because it's cheaper. (must / should)
6. You _____ check out of most hotel rooms by noon if you don't want to pay for another night. (need to / ought to)

B PAIR WORK Imagine you're going to travel abroad. Take turns giving each other advice.

"You must take enough medication for your entire trip."

1. You . . . take enough medication for your entire trip.
2. You . . . take your ATM card with you.
3. You . . . get the necessary vaccinations.
4. You . . . forget to pack your camera.
5. You . . . have a visa to enter some foreign countries.
6. You . . . change money before you go. You can do it when you arrive.

8 PRONUNCIATION Linked sounds with /w/ and /y/

Listen and practice. Notice how some words are linked by a /w/ sound, and other words are linked by a /y/ sound.

/w/
You should know about local conditions.

/w/
You ought to do it right away.

/y/
You shouldn't carry a lot of cash.

/y/
You must be at least 21 years old.

Hit the road! **33**

9 LISTENING A pleasant trip

A Listen to an interview with a spokeswoman from the London Visitor Center. Number the topics she discusses in the correct order from 1 to 4.

a. ☐ money _____
b. ☐ public transportation _____
c. ☐ safety _____
d. ☐ planning a trip _____

B Listen again. Write one piece of advice that she gives for each topic.

C GROUP WORK Which pieces of advice for London apply to your city or town? Which don't? Why and why not?

10 WRITING Have a safe trip.

A Imagine someone is going to visit your town, city, or country. Write an email giving some suggestions for sightseeing activities.

> Dear Michael,
>
> I'm so glad you're coming to visit me in Valparaiso. There are lots of things to see here, and we are going to walk a lot, so bring some comfortable shoes. Don't forget your swimsuit, because I'm planning to take you to Vina del Mar for a day at the beach. It will be warm, so you don't need to pack . . .

Valparaiso, Chile

B PAIR WORK Exchange emails. Is there anything else the visitor needs to know about (food, money, business hours, etc.)?

11 DISCUSSION Around the world

A PAIR WORK You just won a free 30-day trip around the world. Discuss the following questions.

When will you leave and return?
Which direction will you go (east, west, north, or south)?
Where will you choose to stop? Why?
How will you get from place to place?
How long will you stay in each place?

B PAIR WORK What do you need to do before you go? Discuss these topics.

shopping   documents   reservations
packing   money   vaccinations

A: I think we'd better buy new suitcases.
B: Good idea. And we should check the weather before we pack.

Unit 5

12 READING

A Skim the article. Match paragraphs A, B, and C to the photos.

ADVENTURE VACATIONS

Home   About   Vacations   Hot spots   Discounts

A good vacation, for many people, means comfortable accommodations, a great atmosphere, and tasty food. It's a pleasant, relaxing experience. But for some, this type of vacation just isn't enough!
In today's world, many of us have safe, sometimes boring lives. We work, sleep, eat, and watch TV. So more and more people are looking for adventure. They want excitement and danger. They might even want to feel a little afraid!

____ A How about staying on a desert island in the middle of the Indian Ocean? If you want, you can spend your whole vacation completely alone. You'll sleep in a tent and go fishing for your food. Your only company will be the monkeys and lizards. But don't worry. If you get bored, just call the travel company and they'll send a boat to pick you up!

____ B Or how about spending a week in the sub-zero temperatures of the North? You will fly to the Arctic, and the local Sami people will teach you to survive in this very difficult environment. You'll learn how to keep yourself warm and make special snowshoes. You can also go ice-fishing and look after reindeer. You'll even learn how to tell when it is going to snow.

____ C But if the Arctic's too cold, you could try the heat of the jungle instead. Deep in the Amazon rain forest, you'll sleep in the open air. At first, you'll spend a week with local guides. They will train you to do many things, like find food and water or light fires with stones. They will even teach you to pick the tastiest insects for dinner! Then you'll spend a week by yourself with no tent, no extra clothes, and no cell phone. You'll be completely alone – except for the crocodiles and snakes, of course!

B Read the article. Then complete the summary using words from the article.

Nowadays, life can sometimes be a little boring. So, many people are searching for an exciting or dangerous **1)** _____ during their vacations. Some people like the idea of visiting a desert island. There, they spend nights in a **2)** _____ and look for fruit and other plants to eat. If they decide to go to the Arctic instead, they will walk around with unusual **3)** _____ on their feet, and they'll have the experience of taking care of **4)** _____. If they decide to choose a trip to the rain forest, they'll learn many things from **5)** _____, and afterward, they'll live for a whole **6)** _____ completely alone.

C Read the comments of people who are on one of these three trips. Which vacation are they on? Write the letter.

____ 1. "I know what the weather will be like tomorrow."
____ 2. "I haven't seen anybody since the moment I arrived."
____ 3. "My whole body is absolutely freezing!"
____ 4. "I've learned so much these first seven days."
____ 5. "I've had enough now! I'm going to call for help."
____ 6. "I haven't eaten anything like this before!"

D GROUP WORK Which of these three vacations would you be prepared to try? Which would you refuse to go on? Why?

Hit the road! 35

6 Sure! I'll do it.

▶ Discuss common complaints
▶ Make and respond to requests
▶ Apologize

1 SNAPSHOT

FAMILY COMPLAINTS

- ☐ We never have dinner together as a family.
- ☐ Everybody is always arguing about housework.
- ☐ My daughter never takes her headphones off.
- ☐ My father criticizes everything I do.
- ☐ My husband never helps around the house.
- ☐ My kids are always texting their friends.
- ☐ My mother often calls me late at night.
- ☐ My parents don't respect my privacy.
- ☐ My brother never puts his phone away.
- ☐ My wife always brings work home on weekends.

Which complaints seem reasonable? Which ones seem unreasonable? Why?
Do you have similar complaints about anyone in your family? Check (✓) the complaints.
What other complaints do people sometimes have about family members?

2 CONVERSATION I'll turn it off.

A Listen and practice.

Nolan: Please turn down the TV. I have to study.
Ken: I'm sorry. I'll turn it down.
Nolan: It's still too loud.
Ken: All right. I'll turn it off. I'll go watch this show in my room.
Nolan: Thanks.
Ken: No problem.
Nolan: This place is such a mess. Rodrigo, your clothes are all over the place.
Rodrigo: They're not mine. . . . And these books are yours, actually. Why don't you put them away?
Nolan: I'm sorry. I guess I'm kind of nervous about my exam tomorrow.
Rodrigo: That's OK. I know how you feel. Those exams drive me crazy, too.

B Listen to the rest of the conversation. What complaints do Nolan and Rodrigo have about Ken?

3 GRAMMAR FOCUS

Two-part verbs; *will* for responding to requests

With nouns
Turn down the TV.
Turn the TV **down**.
Put away your books.
Put your books **away**.

With pronouns
Turn it **down**.
(NOT: Turn down it.)
Put them **away**.
(NOT: Put away them.)

Requests and responses
Please turn down the music.
 OK. I**'ll** turn it down.
Put away your books, please.
 All right. I**'ll** put them away.

GRAMMAR PLUS see page 137

A Complete the requests with these words. Then compare with a partner.

| your boots | your socks | your jacket | the cat | the trash |
| the TV | ✓ the lights | the magazines | the music | the yard |

1. Turn ___the lights___ off, please.
2. Turn _____ on, please.
3. Please turn _____ down.
4. Pick up _____, please.
5. Please put _____ away.
6. Hang _____ up, please.
7. Please take _____ off.
8. Clean _____ up, please.
9. Please take _____ out.
10. Please let _____ out.

B **PAIR WORK** Take turns making the requests above. Respond with pronouns.

 A: Turn the lights off, please.
 B: No problem. I'll turn them off.

4 PRONUNCIATION Stress in two-part verbs

A Listen and practice. Both words in a two-part verb receive equal stress.

●	●	•	●	●	•	●	●	●	•	●
Pick	up	your	things.	Pick	your	things	up.	Pick	them	up.
Turn	off	the	light.	Turn	the	light	off.	Turn	it	off.

B Write four more requests using the verbs in Exercise 3.
Then practice with a partner. Pay attention to stress.

Sure! I'll do it. **37**

5 WORD POWER Housework

A Find a phrase that is usually paired with each two-part verb. (Some phrases go with more than one verb.) Then add one more phrase for each verb.

| the garbage | the magazines | the microwave | your coat |
| the groceries | the mess | the towels | your laptop |

clean up _____ _____   take out   _____ _____
hang up   _____ _____   throw out _____ _____
pick up   _____ _____   turn off   _____ _____
put away _____ _____   turn on   _____ _____

B What requests can you make in each of these rooms? Write four requests and four excuses. Use two-part verbs.

the kitchen   the living room
the bathroom   the bedroom

C **PAIR WORK** Take turns making the requests you wrote in part B. Respond by giving an excuse.

A: Marabel, please pick up the wet towel you left on your bed.
B: Sorry, I can't pick it up right now. I have to put my new clothes away.

6 LISTENING Helping around the house

A Listen to the results of a survey about family life. Check (✓) the answer to each question. Sometimes more than one answer is possible.

	Men	Women	Boys	Girls
1. Who is the messiest in the house?				
2. Who does most of the work in the kitchen?				
3. Who does the general chores inside and outside the house?				
4. Who worries most about expenses?				

B Listen again. According to the survey, what specific chores do men, women, boys, and girls usually do? Take notes.

C **GROUP WORK** How does your family compare to the survey results? Who helps the most with general chores around the house? Who helps the least?

7 PERSPECTIVES Difficult neighbors

A Match the sentences. Then listen and check your answers. Are all the requests reasonable?

1. "Would you take your garbage out, please?" ___
2. "Would you mind not parking your car in my parking space?" ___
3. "Would you mind turning the music down, please?" ___
4. "Could you close the door behind you and make sure it locks?" ___
5. "Can you keep your cat inside, please?" ___

a. We don't want strangers to enter the building."
b. It often comes into my apartment through the balcony."
c. It can attract insects."
d. The walls are really thin, so the sound goes through to my apartment."
e. I need to park mine there."

B Look at the requests again. Have you ever made similar requests? Has anyone ever asked you to do similar things?

8 GRAMMAR FOCUS

Requests with modals and *Would you mind . . . ?*

Modal + simple form of verb
Can you **keep** your cat inside, please?
Could you **turn** the music **down**, please?
Would you please **park** your car in your space?

***Would you mind . . .* + gerund**
Would you mind keeping your cat inside?
Would you mind turning the music **down**, please?
Would you mind not parking your car in my space?

GRAMMAR PLUS see page 137

A Match the requests in column A with the appropriate responses in column B. Then compare with a partner and practice them. (More than one answer may be possible.)

A
1. Would you mind not using your phone in class? ___
2. Would you mind speaking more quietly? ___
3. Would you please turn on the air conditioner? ___
4. Can you make me a sandwich? ___
5. Can you help me with my homework? ___
6. Could you lend me twenty dollars, please? ___

B
a. Sure, no problem. I'd be glad to.
b. Sorry. We didn't know we were so loud.
c. Sure. Do you want anything to drink?
d. Sorry. I had to talk to my boss.
e. I'm sorry, I can't. I don't have any cash.
f. I'm really sorry, but I'm busy.

B PAIR WORK Take turns making the requests in part A. Give your own responses.

C CLASS ACTIVITY Think of five unusual requests. Go around the class and make your requests. How many people accept? How many refuse?

A: Would you please lend me your car for the weekend?
B: Oh, I'm sorry. I'm going to wash it.

Sure! I'll do it.

9 SPEAKING Apologies

Choose one of the situations below. Take turns making a request to your "neighbor." The "neighbor" should apologize by giving an excuse, admitting a mistake, or making an offer or a promise.

A: Would you mind not making so much noise? It's very late.
B: Oh, I'm sorry. I didn't realize it bothered you.

Different ways to apologize

give an excuse	"I'm sorry. I didn't realize . . ."
admit a mistake	"I forgot I left it there."
make an offer	"I'll take it out right now."
make a promise	"I promise I'll . . ./I'll make sure to . . ."

10 INTERCHANGE 6 I'm terribly sorry.

How good are you at apologizing? Go to Interchange 6 on page 119.

11 WRITING A public message

A Think of a problem that you could have with your neighbors. Write a message explaining the problem and making a request.

> To the person who left a big mess in the laundry room yesterday afternoon: Would you mind cleaning up after you finish your laundry? I fell down and almost broke my leg because the floor was all wet. Thank you.

B PAIR WORK Exchange messages with your classmates. Write a message apologizing for the problem you caused to your "neighbor."

> I'm sorry about the mess in the laundry room. My boss called me, and I had to go back to the office. I'll make sure to clean it up next time.

C GROUP WORK Take turns reading your messages aloud. Do you have similar problems with your neighbors? How do you solve them?

12 READING

A Scan the text. How many of the requests and complaints are about food?

| HOME | WORLD | CULTURE | TRAVEL | BUSINESS | SPORTS | FOOD |

HOTEL MADNESS: THE CRAZY THINGS PEOPLE SAY!

There are about 500,000 hotels around the world. Every day, receptionists, servers, chefs, and managers work in these hotels looking after their guests. Guests often make special requests for things like an extra-large bed or a room with a view of the water. And sometimes people complain when something is not *satisfactory*. In the U.S., around two-thirds of these complaints are about the noise that other guests are making. Sometimes, guests' requests and complaints can make a hotel worker's job almost impossible!

I think I'd look good in that jacket.

Well, sir, we always try to help, but . . .

Here are some very *weird* requests that hotel workers have actually heard:

"Would you mind lending me your suit tomorrow? I have a job interview to go to!"
"Could one of the staff *give* my daughter *a hand* with her homework?"
"Can you please fill my bath with chocolate milk?"
"I'd like chicken for dinner, please, but only the right leg."
"Can you make sure all the strawberries in my cereal are the same size?"

Some hotel guests are also very good at finding (or imagining) problems! These are some of their crazy complaints:

At a London hotel, 40 miles from the coast: "I can't see the ocean from my room."

At a Portuguese hotel: "My bed is way too comfortable. I keep *oversleeping* and missing the best part of the day!"
At a hotel in Spain: "There are too many tasty dishes on the restaurant buffet. I've gained more than 5 pounds!"
To a receptionist in the middle of the night: "I haven't been able to sleep at all! My wife won't stop *snoring*!"
After coming back from a day trip to a water park: "Nobody told us to bring our swimsuits and towels."

So the next time you're at a hotel and the staff look tired, be patient! Maybe they've had a stressful day!

B Read the article. Find the words in *italics* in the article. Then match each word with its meaning.

1. give (somebody) a hand ___
2. satisfactory ___
3. weird ___
4. snoring ___
5. oversleep ___

a. to breathe in a noisy way when asleep
b. help a person do something
c. good enough
d. not wake up early enough
e. very strange

C The sentences below are false. Correct each sentence to make it true.

1. It's common for guests to request a bigger room.
2. One hotel guest asked to borrow an employee's dress.
3. Another guest wanted the fruit at breakfast to be the same color.
4. One person wasn't happy because he kept getting up too early.
5. Someone complained about not taking the right things to go sightseeing.

D PAIR WORK Imagine you are the managers of a hotel. How would you respond to the requests and complaints above? Try to be as polite as you can!

Sure! I'll do it. **41**

Units 5–6 Progress check

SELF-ASSESSMENT

How well can you do these things? Check (✓) the boxes.

I can . . .	Very well	OK	A little
Understand descriptions of people's plans (Ex. 1)	☐	☐	☐
Discuss vacation plans (Ex. 2)	☐	☐	☐
Give travel advice (Ex. 2)	☐	☐	☐
Make and respond to requests (Ex. 3, 4)	☐	☐	☐
Apologize and give excuses (Ex. 3, 4)	☐	☐	☐

1 LISTENING What are your plans?

A Listen to Lily, Tyler, and Abby describe their summer plans. What is each person going to do?

Summer plans	Reason
1. Lily _____	_____
2. Tyler _____	_____
3. Abby _____	_____

B Listen again. What is the reason for each person's choice?

C PAIR WORK What did you do last summer? Listen to your partner and share with the class.

2 DISCUSSION Vacation plans

A GROUP WORK Imagine you are going to go on vacation. Take turns asking and answering these questions.

A: Where are you going to go on your next vacation?
B: I'm going to go to New York.
A: What are you going to do?
B: I'm going to visit the museums. Maybe I'll see a musical on Broadway.
A: Why did you choose that?
B: Well, I want to have a more cultural vacation this year.

B GROUP WORK What should each person do to prepare for his or her vacation? Give each other advice.

3 ROLE PLAY Making excuses

Student A: Your partner was supposed to do some things, but didn't. Look at the pictures and make a request about each one.

Student B: You were supposed to do some things, but didn't. Listen to your partner's requests. Apologize and either agree to the request or give an excuse.

A: Your room is a big mess. Please clean it up.
B: I'm sorry. I forgot about it. I'll clean it up after dinner.

Change roles and try the role play again.

4 GAME Can I ask you a favor?

A Write three requests on separate cards. Put an *X* on the back of two of the cards.

- Can you help me with my homework?
- Could you get me a cup of coffee?
- Would you mind cooking dinner tonight?

B CLASS ACTIVITY Shuffle all the cards together. Take three new cards.

Go around the class and take turns making requests with the cards. Hold up each card so your classmate can see the back.

When answering:

X on the back = refuse the request and give an excuse

No *X* = agree to the request

Can you help me with my homework?

I'm sorry, I can't. I'm . . .

WHAT'S NEXT?

Look at your Self-assessment again. Do you need to review anything?

7 What do you use this for?

▸ Describe uses and purposes of technology
▸ Give suggestions

1 SNAPSHOT

Inventions We Can't Live Without

- ☐ smartphones
- ☐ digital cameras
- ☐ Internet
- ☐ e-readers
- ☐ tablet computers
- ☐ streaming TV
- ☐ robots
- ☐ 3-D printers
- ☐ driverless cars
- ☐ GPS technology
- ☐ drones
- ☐ Wi-Fi

How long have the inventions above been around in your country?
How was life different before them?
Check (✓) three inventions you couldn't live without. Compare with a partner.

2 PERSPECTIVES Smartphone usage

A How do you use your smartphone? Listen and respond to the statements.

I use my smartphone . . .	Often	Sometimes	Hardly ever	Never
to send messages	☐	☐	☐	☐
for watching videos	☐	☐	☐	☐
to take photos	☐	☐	☐	☐
to post on social media sites	☐	☐	☐	☐
for doing school assignments	☐	☐	☐	☐
to send emails	☐	☐	☐	☐
to shop online	☐	☐	☐	☐
to check the weather	☐	☐	☐	☐
to read e-books	☐	☐	☐	☐
for listening to music	☐	☐	☐	☐

B **PAIR WORK** Compare your answers. Are your answers similar or different?

3 GRAMMAR FOCUS

Infinitives and gerunds for uses and purposes

Infinitives
I use my cell phone **to send** messages.
Some people use their phones **to watch** videos.
People often use their phones **to take** photos.

Gerunds
I use my cell phone **for sending** messages.
Some people use their phones **for watching** videos.
People often use their phones **for taking** photos.

GRAMMAR PLUS see page 138

A PAIR WORK What do you know about this technology? Complete the sentences in column A with information from column B. Use infinitives and gerunds. (More than one combination is possible.)

A
1. Many people use tablet computers . . .
2. You can use your smartphone . . .
3. Engineers use 3-D printers . . .
4. People can use the Internet . . .
5. Companies sometimes use robots . . .
6. The police use drones . . .

B
look for criminals.
perform dangerous tasks.
get directions.
make car parts.
make video calls.
learn languages.

Many people use tablet computers to make video calls.
Many people use tablet computers for making video calls.

B PAIR WORK Think of one other use for the items in column A.

"Paparazzi use drones to spy on celebrities."

C GROUP WORK List some unexpected uses for these new and old items. Compare your answers with the whole class. Who came up with the most uses?

a smartphone   a paper clip   a webcam   a pencil   invisible tape   an old CD

"You can use your smartphone for driving your car."

4 PRONUNCIATION Syllable stress

A Listen and practice. Notice which syllable has the main stress.

●••	•●•	••●
Internet	invention	engineer
messages	assignment	DVD
digital	computer	recommend

B Where is the stress in these words? Add them to the columns in part A. Then listen and check.

directions   driverless   entertain   equipment   media   understand

5 WORD POWER Plugged in

A Complete the chart with words and phrases from the list. Add one more to each category. Then compare with a partner.

✓ computer whiz	hacker	check in for a flight	geek
computer crash	edit photos	download apps	software bugs
flash drive	identity theft	make international phone calls	frozen screen
smart devices	early adopter	solar-powered batteries	phone charger

Problems with technology	Gadgets and devices	People who are "into" technology	Things to do online
		computer whiz	

B GROUP WORK Discuss some of the positive and negative consequences of living in a connected world.

– Have you ever had any of the problems mentioned in part A? What happened? What did you do?
– Do you have any smart devices? Which ones? How do they help you? How much do you depend on them?
– Do you have any friends who never put their phone away? Is anyone in your family addicted to new technologies? Are you?
– What is one gadget you would really like to have? Why?
– Is identity theft a problem where you live? What about hackers? How do you protect against them?

6 LISTENING They've thought of everything!

A Listen to two people talk about the best apps for travel. Check (✓) the four app categories. (There are two extra categories.)

☐ safety _____
☐ packing _____
☐ music _____
☐ transportation _____
☐ attractions _____
☐ hotel _____

B Listen again. What can you use the apps for? Write the uses next to the categories you checked above.

C PAIR WORK What are your favorite apps? Discuss and share with the class.

46 Unit 7

7 CONVERSATION What do I do now?

A Listen and practice.

Justin: I can't believe my phone's frozen again.
Allie: How long have you had it?
Justin: About a year. It's not that old.
Allie: Maybe someone hacked it.
Justin: Really? You think so?
Allie: No, I'm just kidding. It's probably just a virus.
Justin: Oh. So what do I do now?
Allie: First, you'd better install a good antivirus app. And be sure to update it.
Justin: OK, I'll download one now. What else should I do?
Allie: Well, don't forget to reset all your passwords.
Justin: That's a good idea. I never remember to change my passwords.
Allie: One more thing. Try not to use public Wi-Fi networks.
Justin: You're right. I have to learn to be more careful.

B Listen to the rest of the conversation. What else does Justin want help with? What does Allie suggest?

8 GRAMMAR FOCUS

Imperatives and infinitives for giving suggestions

Be sure to update the app.
Make sure to charge your phone.
Remember to back up your files.

Don't forget to reset your passwords.
Try not to use public Wi-Fi networks.

GRAMMAR PLUS see page 138

A Look at the suggestions. Rewrite them using these phrases. Then compare with a partner.

Make sure to . . .   Try to . . .   Remember to . . .
Be sure not to . . .   Try not to . . .   Don't forget to . . .

1. a. Before using an electronic safe, you have to reset the passcode.
   b. You should check if it's locked after you close it.
2. a. Don't get your phone wet or it might not work anymore.
   b. It's important to back up your contacts and other important information.
3. a. You must set your alarm system each time you leave home.
   b. Don't use your birthday as a code.
4. a. You ought to keep the lenses of your digital camera clean.
   b. It's important to keep the lens cap on when you're not taking photos.

B **PAIR WORK** Take turns giving other suggestions for using the items in part A.

What do you use this for?

9 LISTENING Smart suggestions

▶ **A** Listen to people give suggestions for using three of these things. Number them 1, 2, and 3. (There are two extra things.)

☐ portable speaker

☐ GPS system

☐ flash drive

☐ smartphone

☐ ATM card

▶ **B** Listen again. Write two suggestions you hear for each thing. Then compare with a partner.

1. _____   _____
2. _____   _____
3. _____   _____

C **PAIR WORK** What do you know about the other two things in part A? Give suggestions about them.

"Be sure to buy one with lots of memory."

10 INTERCHANGE 7 Free advice

Give your classmates some advice. Go to Interchange 7 on page 121.

11 WRITING A message

A Imagine your brother is coming over for dinner, but you are going to be busy all day. Your roommate has agreed to help you. Think of three things you need help with. Then write a message with instructions.

B **GROUP WORK** Take turns reading your messages aloud. Did you ask for similar favors?

> Hi, Melissa. Thanks a lot for your help. Please remember to do these three things. First, make sure to buy some groceries. The shopping list is on the refrigerator. Also, please don't forget to . . .

12 READING

A Skim the article. What is the sharing economy? What three examples does the article give?

THE SHARING ECONOMY – GOOD FOR EVERYBODY?

Modern technology has made it easier for ordinary people to rent things or services to others. With the click of an app, we can find almost anything. It could be a new dress to wear on the weekend, or someone to clean your house. This is the sharing economy, and it is now a profitable $20 billion-a-year business. But some people are now asking: Just how good is it for society in general?

Not long ago, when people went on vacation, they usually stayed in a hotel. Today they have the choice of staying in someone's private house. They pay less, but what effect does this have on the hotel industry and the wider economy? Hotels receive fewer guests, but they still have to pay salaries to their employees and taxes to the government. Many people who rent out rooms do not. So the government gets less money, and some hotels might even close down.

Then there are car-sharing sites. Instead of using your own car for a long trip you can get a ride with someone for a small fee. Some people argue this is better for the environment, since fewer cars on the roads means less pollution. But how many people choose to use these sites rather than taking the bus or the train? Public transportation is, after all, much kinder to the environment than cars.

Many sites offer cooking services. Instead of going to a restaurant, you can use an app to order dishes from people in your neighborhood.

There is even a site where you can buy leftover food that people haven't eaten! This is sure to save you time and money. But is it risky? Can you trust the people cooking your food? Restaurants have to follow strict regulations to make sure their food is safe to eat.

There is no doubt that the sharing economy is growing. Some economists think it will be worth $335 billion by 2025. As new technology makes sharing food, accommodation, and transportation easier all the time, the question of "Is it fair?" will remain.

B Read the article. Find the words in *italics* below. Then circle the meaning of each word.
1. When a business is *profitable*, it **makes / loses** money.
2. *Taxes* are money that people **give to / receive from** the government.
3. If something is *risky*, it's **dangerous / safe**.
4. *Regulations* are **rules / people** that control how we do things.
5. When something is *fair*, everybody has **equal / different** opportunities.

C Answer the questions.
1. How much is the sharing economy worth nowadays?
2. What is the advantage of staying in a private house instead of a hotel?
3. Why is car sharing less damaging to the environment?
4. What is better for the environment than car sharing?
5. How can buying food from non-professionals be risky?

D Do you use any of these sharing-economy services? Are they ever risky? Do you think they are fair?

What do you use this for?

8 Time to celebrate!

▶ Discuss holidays and special occasions
▶ Describe celebrations, annual events, and customs

1 SNAPSHOT

HOLIDAYS AND FESTIVALS

Day of the Dead
November 2nd
Mexicans make playful skeleton sculptures and bake *pan de muerto* – bread of the dead.

Thanksgiving
November
In the United States, families get together, have a traditional meal, and give thanks for life and health.

Saint Patrick's Day
March 17th
People of Irish background wear green to celebrate their culture with parades, dancing, parties, and special foods.

Chinese New Year
January or February
Chinese people celebrate the lunar new year with fireworks and dragon dances.

Do you celebrate these or similar holidays in your country?
What other special days do you have?
What's your favorite holiday or festival?

2 WORD POWER Ways to celebrate

A Which word or phrase is not usually paired with each verb?
Put a line through it. Then compare with a partner.

1. eat	candy	sweets	~~a mask~~
2. give	presents	a celebration	money
3. go to	decorations	a wedding	a party
4. have a	picnic	beach	meal
5. play	games	candles	music
6. send	cards	flowers	a barbecue
7. visit	relatives	food	close friends
8. watch	a birthday	a parade	fireworks
9. wear	costumes	invitations	traditional clothes

B **PAIR WORK** Do you do any of the things in part A as part of a cultural or family celebration? When? Tell your partner.

3 PERSPECTIVES Favorite celebrations

A Listen to these comments about special days of the year. Match them to the correct pictures.

___ 1. "My favorite celebration is Mother's Day. It's a day when my husband and my kids make pancakes for me – just like I used to make for my mom – and I get to have breakfast in bed."

___ 2. "February 14th is the day when people give cards and presents to the ones they love. I'm really looking forward to Valentine's Day! I already have a gift for my boyfriend."

___ 3. "New Year's Eve is a night when I have fun with my friends. We usually have a big party. We stay up all night and then go out for breakfast in the morning."

a   b   c

B **PAIR WORK** What do you like about each celebration in part A?

4 GRAMMAR FOCUS

Relative clauses of time

Mother's Day is **a day**	**when** my kids make pancakes for me.
February 14th is **the day**	**when** people give cards to the ones they love.
New Year's Eve is **a night**	**when** I have fun with my friends.

GRAMMAR PLUS see page 139

A How much do you know about these times? Complete the sentences in column A with information from column B. Then compare with a partner.

A
1. Mother's Day is a day when _____
2. New Year's Eve is a night when _____
3. April Fools' Day is a day when _____
4. Valentine's Day is a day when _____
5. Labor Day is a day when _____
6. Summer is a time when _____

B
a. people sometimes play tricks on friends.
b. people celebrate their mothers.
c. many people like to go to the beach.
d. people in many countries honor workers.
e. people express their love to someone.
f. people have parties with family and friends.

B Complete these sentences with your own information. Then compare with a partner.

Winter is the season . . .
Birthdays are days . . .
Spring is the time of year . . .
Children's Day is a day . . .
July and August are the months . . .
A wedding anniversary is a time . . .

Time to celebrate!

5 LISTENING Time for Carnival!

▶ **A** Listen to Vanessa talk about her trip to Carnival in Brazil. Write three facts about Carnival that she mentions.

▶ **B** Listen again and answer these questions about Vanessa's experience.

Why did she have to book her hotel six months early?
What happened when Vanessa got lost?
What was her favorite thing about Carnival? Why?

C PAIR WORK Think of another famous celebration that is similar to Carnival. Describe it to the class. They will try to guess the celebration.

Carnival in Brazil

6 SPEAKING Favorite holidays

A PAIR WORK Choose your three favorite holidays. Tell your partner why you like each one.

A: I really like Independence Day.
B: What do you like about it?
A: It's a day when we watch parades and fireworks.
B: Do you do anything special?
A: We usually have a barbecue. My father makes burgers, and my mother makes her special potato salad.

B CLASS ACTIVITY Take a class vote. What are the most popular holidays in your class?

7 WRITING An online entry

A Write an entry for a travel website about a festival or celebration where you live. When is it? How do people celebrate it? What should a visitor see and do?

> Obon is an annual event when Japanese people commemorate their ancestors. They visit and clean the graves of their dead relatives. People put candles in lanterns and float them on rivers. There are neighborhood dances at parks, gardens, and . . .
>
> read more

B PAIR WORK Read your partner's entry. What do you like about it? Can you suggest anything to improve it?

Unit 8

8 CONVERSATION A traditional wedding

▶ **A** Listen and practice.

JULIA Is this a picture from your wedding, Anusha?

ANUSHA Yes. We had the ceremony in India.

JULIA And was this your wedding dress?

ANUSHA Yes. It's a sari, actually. In India, when women get married, they usually wear a brightly colored sari, not a white dress.

JULIA It's beautiful! So, what are weddings like in India?

ANUSHA Well, in some traditions, after the groom arrives, the bride and groom exchange garlands of flowers. We did that. But we didn't do some other traditional things.

JULIA Oh? Like what?

ANUSHA Well, before the wedding, the bride's female relatives usually have a party to celebrate. But I'm an only child, and I don't have any female cousins, so we skipped that.

JULIA That makes sense. You know, I have heard about this one tradition . . . When the groom takes off his shoes, the bride's sisters steal them! I guess you didn't do that, either?

ANUSHA Oh, no, we did that part. My mom stole them!

▶ **B** Listen to the rest of the conversation.
What does Anusha say about her wedding reception?

9 PRONUNCIATION Stress and rhythm

▶ **A** Listen and practice. Notice how stressed words and syllables occur with a regular rhythm.

●　　●　　●　　●　●　●　●

When women get married, they usually wear a brightly colored sari.

▶ **B** Listen to the stress and rhythm in these sentences. Then practice them.

1. After the groom arrives, the bride and groom exchange garlands of flowers.
2. Before the wedding, the bride's female relatives usually have a party to celebrate.
3. When the groom takes off his shoes, the bride's sisters steal them.

Time to celebrate!

10 GRAMMAR FOCUS

▶ Adverbial clauses of time

When women get married,   they usually wear a brightly colored sari.
After the groom arrives,   the bride and groom exchange garlands of flowers.
Before the wedding,   the bride's female relatives usually have a party to celebrate.

GRAMMAR PLUS see page 139

A What do you know about wedding customs in North America? Complete these sentences with the information below.

1. Before a man and woman get married, they usually ___
2. When a couple gets engaged, the man often ___
3. Right after a couple gets engaged, they usually ___
4. When a woman gets married, she usually ___
5. When guests go to a wedding, they almost always ___
6. Right after a couple gets married, they usually ___

a. wears a long white dress and a veil.
b. go on a short trip called a "honeymoon."
c. give the bride and groom gifts or some money.
d. gives the woman an engagement ring.
e. begin to plan the wedding.
f. date each other for a year or more.

B **PAIR WORK** What happens when people get married in your country? Tell your partner by completing the statements in part A with your own information. Pay attention to stress and rhythm.

11 INTERCHANGE 8 It's worth celebrating.

How do your classmates celebrate special occasions? Go to Interchange 8 on page 122.

12 SPEAKING My personal traditions

A **GROUP WORK** How do you usually celebrate the dates below? Share your personal traditions with your classmates.

your birthday   New Year's Eve   your country's national day   your favorite holiday

A: On my birthday, I always wear new clothes, and I often have a party. What about you?
B: I usually celebrate my birthday with my family. We have a special meal and some relatives come over.
C: I used to celebrate my birthday at home, but now I usually go out with friends.

B **CLASS ACTIVITY** Tell the class the most interesting traditions you talked about in your group. Do you share any common traditions? Did you use to celebrate those dates the same way when you were younger?

13 READING

A Skim the article. Which of these phrases could be a title for this article?

The best New Year's resolutions   New Year's traditions around the world
How to host a New Year's Eve party

Out with the Old, In with THE NEW

It's midnight on New Year's Eve. Clocks are striking twelve as people welcome in the coming year and say goodbye to the old. It's a time when people wish for good luck in the future and forget bad things in the past. Around the world, people do different things to help their wishes come true. Some of <u>them</u> might surprise you.

Food is often central to New Year's customs. In Ireland, they hit the walls and doors of their houses with loaves of bread. They hope <u>this</u> will make good luck enter the house and bad luck leave it. The Spanish and the Mexicans eat twelve grapes in twelve seconds – <u>one</u> for luck in each of the coming months. Eating grapes so fast isn't easy, but it's fun and often messy!

Colors are important, too. Brazilians, for example, choose their clothes very carefully – for peace they wear white, yellow might bring success, and red means love is in the air! The Chinese believe red brings good luck, so they like to dress in this color, too. They also give family members and friends red envelopes containing money.

Some people destroy things on New Year's Eve because they want to forget the past. In Ecuador and Colombia, people make a dummy and fill it with sawdust, newspaper, or old clothes. <u>They</u> dress it, put a mask on it, and name it after someone famous or a friend or family member. Then they burn it.

And some customs have no reason at all; <u>they</u> just develop over time. On New Year's Eve in Germany, several TV stations show a short black-and-white movie called *Dinner for One*. It's a comedy in English, starring English actors. Nobody knows why they do this, not even the Germans!

B Read the article. Check (✓) True or False for each statement about New Year's customs. Then correct each false statement.

	True	False	
1. In Ireland, people eat loaves of bread for good luck.	☐	☐	
2. They eat apples for good luck in Spain.	☐	☐	
3. In China, people change the color of their doors.	☐	☐	
4. In Colombia, they burn a doll with old things inside.	☐	☐	
5. In Germany, people watch *Dinner for One* because it's about New Year's Eve.	☐	☐	

C What do the underlined words in the article refer to? Write the correct word.

1. them _____   3. one _____   5. they _____
2. this _____   4. They _____

D What do people in your country do for the New Year? What is your favorite New Year's tradition?

Time to celebrate! **55**

Units 7–8 Progress check

SELF-ASSESSMENT

How well can you do these things? Check (✓) the boxes.

I can . . .	Very well	OK	A little
Describe uses and purposes of objects (Ex. 1)	☐	☐	☐
Give instructions and suggestions (Ex. 2)	☐	☐	☐
Describe holidays and special occasions (Ex. 3, 5)	☐	☐	☐
Understand descriptions of customs (Ex. 4, 5)	☐	☐	☐
Ask and answer questions about celebrations and customs (Ex. 5)	☐	☐	☐

1 GAME Guess my object.

A PAIR WORK Think of five familiar objects. Write a short description of each object's use and purpose. Don't write the name of the objects.

> It's electronic. It's small. It connects to the Internet.
> You wear it. It communicates with your phone.

B GROUP WORK Take turns reading your descriptions and guessing the objects. Keep score. Who guessed the most items correctly? Who wrote the best descriptions?

2 ROLE PLAY It's all under control.

Student A: Choose one situation below. Decide on the details and answer Student B's questions. Then get some suggestions.

Start like this: *I'm really nervous. I'm . . .*

giving a speech
What is it about?
Where is it?
How many people will be there?

going on a job interview
What's the job?
What are the responsibilities?
Who is interviewing you?

taking my driving test
When is it?
How long is it?
Have you prepared?

Student B: Student A is telling you about a situation. Ask the appropriate questions above. Then give some suggestions.

Change roles and try the role play again.

useful expressions	
Try to . . .	Try not to . . .
Remember to . . .	Be sure to . . .
Don't forget to . . .	Make sure to . . .

3 SPEAKING Unofficial holidays

A PAIR WORK Choose one of these holidays or create your own. Then write a description of the holiday. Answer the questions below.

Buy Nothing Day

National Day of Unplugging

World Smile Day

What is the name of the holiday? When is it?
How do you celebrate it?

Buy Nothing Day is a day when you can't buy anything. It's a day to think about what we consume, what we really need, and how much money we waste.

B GROUP WORK Read your description to the group. Then vote on the best holiday.

4 LISTENING Marriage customs around the world

▶ **A** Listen to two people discuss a book about marriage customs. Match each country to the title that describes its marriage custom.

1. Sweden ___
2. China ___
3. Paraguay ___
4. Germany ___

a. *Fighting for Love*
b. *Dishes for Good Luck*
c. *Kisses for Guests*
d. *Tears of Happiness*

▶ **B** Listen again. Complete the sentences to describe the custom.

1. When the groom leaves the table, _____.
2. One month before the wedding, _____.
3. When they want to marry the same man, _____.
4. After the guests bring the dishes to the couple, _____.

C PAIR WORK Think of some marriage customs from your country. How are they similar to these customs? How are they different?

5 DISCUSSION Just married

GROUP WORK Talk about marriage in your country. Ask these questions and others of your own.

How old are people when they get married?
What happens after a couple gets engaged?
What happens during the ceremony?
What do the bride and groom wear?
What kinds of food is served at the reception?
What kinds of gifts do people usually give?

WHAT'S NEXT?

Look at your Self-assessment again. Do you need to review anything?

9 Only time will tell.

▶ Discuss life in different times
▶ Discuss consequences

1 SNAPSHOT

	PAST	PRESENT	FUTURE
EDUCATION	• printed books • blackboard	• e-books • digital content	• virtual classrooms • learning pills
WORK	• time clocks • assembly line	• frequent career changes • multiple workplaces	• intelligent robots • 2-hour work day
TRANSPORTATION	• steam trains • ocean liners	• non-polluting vehicles • shared cars	• driverless cars • teleportation

Which of these changes are the most important? How have they affected the way we live?
Do you think any of the future developments could happen in your lifetime?
Can you think of two other developments that could happen in the future?

2 CONVERSATION That's a thing of the past!

A Listen and practice.

Tom: I hardly recognize our old neighborhood. A few years ago, there were just houses around here.

Mia: I know. They're building a lot of new apartments. The whole neighborhood's different.

Tom: Remember the little burger restaurant we used to go to after school, Hamburger Heaven?

Mia: Of course . . . Now it's another office tower. And I hear they're tearing down our high school. They're going to build a shopping mall.

Tom: That's such a shame. Pretty soon the neighborhood will just be a bunch of malls. And maybe there won't be any schools anymore.

Mia: Probably not. Kids will study from their computers anywhere they want.

Tom: So they won't hang out with their friends after school? That's too bad. I enjoyed meeting our friends at that burger place after class.

Mia: Seriously? That's a thing of the past! Nowadays, kids only meet online.

B Listen to the rest of the conversation. What else has changed in their neighborhood?

58

3 GRAMMAR FOCUS

Time contrasts

Past

A few years ago, there **were** just houses here.

We **used to go** to a burger place after class every day.

In the past, kids **used to hang out** with friends after school.

Present

These days, they**'re building** lots of apartments.

Today, people **order** food from their phones.

Nowadays, kids only **meet** online.

Future

Soon, there **will be** apartment blocks everywhere.

In the future, restaurants **might not exist**.

In a few years, we **are going to have** virtual friends.

GRAMMAR PLUS see page 140

A Complete the sentences in column A with the appropriate information from column B. Then compare with a partner.

A
1. In the early 1990s, ___
2. Before the airplane, ___
3. Before there were supermarkets, ___
4. In many companies these days, ___
5. In most big cities nowadays, ___
6. In many schools today, ___
7. In the next 100 years, ___
8. Sometime in the near future, ___

B
a. students have their own tablets.
b. pollution is becoming a serious problem.
c. there will probably be cities in space.
d. few people had cell phones.
e. people used to shop at small grocery stores.
f. women still receive lower salaries than men.
g. doctors might find a cure for the common cold.
h. ocean liners were the only way to travel across the Atlantic.

B Complete four of the phrases in part A, column A, with your own ideas. Then compare with a partner.

4 PRONUNCIATION Intonation in statements with time phrases

A Listen and practice. Notice the intonation in these statements beginning with a time phrase.

In the past, few women went to college.

Today, there are more women than men in college in the United States.

In the future, women all over the world will go to college.

B PAIR WORK Complete these statements with your own information. Then read your statements to a partner. Pay attention to intonation.

As a child, I used to . . .
Five years ago, I . . .
Nowadays, I . . .

These days, . . .
In five years, I'll . . .
In ten years, I might . . .

5 LISTENING On the other side of the world

A Listen to Katie talk to her grandfather about an upcoming trip. Check (✓) the three concerns her grandfather has about the trip.

Concern
1. ☐ language   ☐ transportation
2. ☐ meeting people   ☐ money
3. ☐ communication   ☐ food

Katie's response
_____
_____
_____

B Listen again. Write what Katie says in response to these concerns.

C PAIR WORK What other problems might someone experience when they travel to another country? How might these problems change in the future?

6 SPEAKING Not anymore.

GROUP WORK How have things changed? How will things be different in the future? Choose four of these topics. Then discuss the questions below.

communications	education	housing
entertainment	fashion	shopping
environment	food	traveling
health		

What was it like in the past?
What is it like today?
What will it be like in the future?

A: In the past, people cooked all their meals at home.
B: Not anymore. Nowadays, we eat takeout food all the time.
C: In the future, . . .

7 WRITING He's changed a lot.

A PAIR WORK Interview your partner about his or her past, present, and hopes for the future.

B Write a paragraph describing how your partner has changed. Make some predictions about the future. Don't write your partner's name.

> This person came to our school about two years ago. He used to be a little shy in class, and he didn't have many friends. Now, he's on the basketball team and he is very popular. He's a very talented player and, someday, he'll play on the national team. He'll be famous and very rich. I think he'll . . .

C CLASS ACTIVITY Read your paragraph to the class. Can they guess who it is about?

8 PERSPECTIVES Making the big bucks

A Listen to some possible consequences of getting a high-paying job. Check (✓) the statements you agree with.

If you get a high-paying job, . . .

- ☐ your friends might ask you for a loan.
- ☐ you'll have a lot of money to spend.
- ☐ more people may want to be your friend.
- ☐ you won't have much time for your family.
- ☐ you'll be able to buy anything you want.
- ☐ you won't be able to take long vacations.
- ☐ you'll have to pay higher taxes.
- ☐ you won't have to worry about the future.

B **PAIR WORK** Look at the statements again. Which are advantages of getting a high-paying job? Which are disadvantages?

"The first one is a disadvantage. I'd like to help my friends, but I wouldn't like to lend them money."

9 GRAMMAR FOCUS

Conditional sentences with *if* clauses

Possible situation (present)	Consequence (future with *will*, *may*, or *might*)
If you **get** a high-paying job,	you**'ll have** more cash to spend.
If you **have** more cash to spend,	you**'ll be able to buy** anything you want.
If you **can buy** anything you want,	you **won't save** your money.
If you **don't save** your money,	you **may have to get** a weekend job.
If you **have to get** a weekend job,	you **might not have** any free time.

GRAMMAR PLUS *see page 140*

A Match the *if* clauses in column A with the appropriate consequences from column B. Then compare with a partner.

A
1. If you eat less fast food, ____
2. If you walk to work every day, ____
3. If you don't get enough sleep, ____
4. If you change jobs, ____
5. If you don't study regularly, ____
6. If you travel abroad, ____

B
a. you may not learn to speak fluently.
b. you might feel a lot healthier.
c. you'll stay in shape without joining a gym.
d. you'll be able to experience a new culture.
e. you won't be able to stay awake in class.
f. you may not like it better than your old one.

B Add your own consequences to the *if* clauses in column A. Then practice with a partner.

"If you eat less fast food, you will probably live longer."

Only time will tell.

10 WORD POWER Collocations

A PAIR WORK Find phrases from the list that usually go with each verb. (Sometimes more than one answer is possible.)

a club	a gym	in shape	money	tired
✓ a degree	a living	into college	stressed	work experience
a group	energy	jealous	time	your own money

earn _a degree_ _____ _____
get _____ _____ _____
join _____ _____ _____
spend _____ _____ _____
feel _____ _____ _____

B GROUP WORK Share your answers with the group. Can you add one more phrase to each verb?

11 SPEAKING Who knows what will happen?

A GROUP WORK Choose three possible events from below. One student completes an event with a consequence. The next student adds a consequence. Suggest at least five consequences.

fall in love   get a part-time job
join a gym   move to a foreign country
study very hard

If you fall in love, you'll probably want to get married.

If you get married, you'll have to earn your own money.

If you want to earn your own money, you'll need to get a job.

If you get a job, you may spend less time at the gym.

If you spend less time at the gym, you won't keep in shape.

B CLASS ACTIVITY Who has the most interesting consequences for each event?

12 INTERCHANGE 9 Cause and effect

Give your opinion about some issues. Go to Interchange 9 on page 123.

13 READING

A Scan the article. Where is Aguaviva? Who is Luis Bricio?

AGUAVIVA: FIGHTING FOR A FUTURE

Twenty years ago, Aguaviva, a small village in the north of Spain, was dying. Young people wanted more opportunities, so they moved away to the cities. By 1991, there were only 618 people left, and most of them were old. Many of the houses were empty and falling down, and the local school had very few children. Aguaviva's future looked dark.

In 2000, the mayor, Luis Bricio, decided something had to change. He wondered, "How can I bring this place back to life?" He knew the village needed people, but from where? Then he had a brilliant idea. He flew 6,300 miles to Buenos Aires and started telling everyone about Aguaviva. He spoke on the radio and put advertisements in newspapers. The ads said, "If you are married with two children under the age of 12, we'll offer you a home, a job, free health care and education for at least five years." The following year, he did the same thing in Romania.

Many families accepted the offer and Aguaviva began to change. The village school went from having 37 students to more than 80 in three years. The sound of children shouting and playing has made the local people feel so much younger. The economy began to improve, too. There was work for builders repairing the old houses, and a factory making electrical parts for cars opened.

Of course, not everything was easy. The people from Buenos Aires were used to a big city, so living in a small village with little public transportation was difficult at first. The Romanians had to learn a new language. And they all missed their family and friends back home. But everybody had new opportunities, too. Before, many of the parents had worried about finding a job and having enough money to look after their children. After moving to Spain, their future looked brighter. Many of them thought, "We're going to stay here for many years – this place will be our home."

B Read the article. Then answer the questions.

1. Why did young people start leaving Aguaviva?
2. How did Luis Bricio try to attract people to Aguaviva?
3. How did the school change after the year 2000?
4. What kinds of new jobs were there in Aguaviva?
5. What problems did the families from Argentina and Romania have?

C Who would make the following comments? Choose the correct words from the box.

| Luis Bricio | young people from Aguaviva |
| elderly people from Aguaviva | new immigrants |

1. "I'm not going back home because life is better here." _____
2. "I can't stay here. There are no jobs for people of my age." _____
3. "I'm going to make this village a better place." _____
4. "I love having all these kids around me – I don't feel so old." _____

D Do you think Luis Bricio had a good idea? Would you move to a place like this? What would you miss most about home?

Only time will tell.

10 I like working with people.

▶ Discuss job skills
▶ Discuss kinds of jobs

1 SNAPSHOT

21ST CENTURY SKILLS

☐ Can you use technology to find the information you need?
☐ Can you evaluate the information you find?
☐ Do you work well with different kinds of people?
☐ Can you communicate with people from different cultures?
☐ Are you good at analyzing and solving problems?
☐ Can you develop new ideas?
☐ Do you enjoy learning new things?
☐ Can you teach others how to do things?

21st century life citizen skills creativity successful technology digital effective global ability thinking knowledge information responsibility network collaborate critical fluency effective flexibility

Which of these skills do you think are most important for work? in life? Why?
Check (✓) the skills that you think you have.
Look at the skills you checked. What jobs do you think you might be good at?

2 CONVERSATION I love playing video games.

▶ **A** Listen and practice.

Mai: What are you doing this summer?
Jeff: Nothing much. I'm broke. I need to find a job!
Mai: So do I. Have you seen anything interesting?
Jeff: No, not yet.
Mai: Why don't you get a job at your uncle's restaurant?
Jeff: No way. They're open evenings and weekends, and I hate working on weekends.
Mai: Well, I don't mind working on weekends. Besides, I really enjoy working with people. Do you think he would give me a job?
Jeff: Why don't you go over this weekend and talk to him?
Mai: Yeah. I'll do that. Oh, I found one for you: video game tester.
Jeff: That sounds like fun. I love playing video games. I'll check that one out.

▶ **B** Listen to the rest of the conversation. What is one problem with the job? What does Jeff decide to do?

3 GRAMMAR FOCUS

▶ **Gerunds; short responses**

Affirmative statements with gerunds

	Agree	Disagree
I love **playing** video games.	So do I.	I don't.
I hate **working** on weekends.	So do I.	Really? I like it.
I'm good at **solving** problems.	So am I.	Oh, I'm not.

Negative statements with gerunds

I don't mind **working** evenings.	Neither do I.	I do.
I'm not good at **selling**.	Neither am I.	Well, I am.
I can't stand **commuting**.	Neither can I.	Oh, I don't mind it.

Other verbs or phrases followed by gerunds

like
enjoy
be interested in

GRAMMAR PLUS see page 141

A PAIR WORK Match the phrases in columns A and B to make statements about yourself. Then take turns reading your sentences and giving short responses.

A
1. I can't stand ___
2. I'm not very good at ___
3. I'm good at ___
4. I don't like ___
5. I hate ___
6. I'm interested in ___
7. I don't mind ___
8. I enjoy ___

B
a. working the night shift.
b. solving other people's problems.
c. working alone.
d. sitting in long meetings.
e. working on weekends.
f. speaking in public.
g. managing my time.
h. learning foreign languages.

A: I can't stand sitting in long meetings.
B: Neither can I.

B GROUP WORK Complete the phrases in column A with your own information. Then take turns reading your statements. Ask questions to get more information.

4 PRONUNCIATION Unreleased and released /t/ and /d/

▶ **A** Listen and practice. Notice that when the sound /t/ or /d/ at the end of a word is followed by a consonant, it's unreleased. When it is followed by a vowel sound, it's released.

Unreleased
She's not good at dealing with stress.
I hate working on Sundays.
You need to manage money well.

Released
He's not a good artist.
They really hate it!
I need a cup of coffee.

B PAIR WORK Write three sentences starting with *I'm not very good at* and *I don't mind*. Then practice the sentences. Pay attention to the unreleased and released sounds /t/ and /d/.

I like working with people.

5 SPEAKING Do what you love.

A PAIR WORK How does your partner feel about doing these things? Interview your partner. Check (✓) his or her answers.

How do you feel about . . . ?	I enjoy it.	I don't mind it.	I hate it.
dealing with the public	☐	☐	☐
working alone	☐	☐	☐
being part of a team	☐	☐	☐
meeting deadlines	☐	☐	☐
leading a team	☐	☐	☐
working on weekends	☐	☐	☐
learning new skills	☐	☐	☐
doing the same thing every day	☐	☐	☐
traveling	☐	☐	☐
making decisions	☐	☐	☐
helping people	☐	☐	☐
solving problems	☐	☐	☐

B PAIR WORK Look back at the information in part A. Suggest a job for your partner.

A: You enjoy dealing with the public, and you hate working alone. You'd be a good salesperson.
B: But I hate working on weekends.
A: Maybe you could . . .

6 LISTENING My ideal career

A Listen to people talk about the kind of work they are looking for. Then check (✓) each person's ideal job.

1. Alex
   ☐ architect
   ☐ accountant
   ☐ teacher

2. Evelyn
   ☐ banker
   ☐ doctor
   ☐ lawyer

3. Edward
   ☐ marine biologist
   ☐ songwriter
   ☐ flight attendant

B Listen again. Write two reasons each person gives for his or her ideal job.

1. Alex _____
2. Evelyn _____
3. Edward _____

7 INTERCHANGE 10 You're hired.

Choose the right person for the job. Go to Interchange 10 on page 124.

8 WORD POWER Personality traits

A Which of these adjectives are positive (**P**)? Which are negative (**N**)?

creative	P	impatient	
critical		level-headed	
disorganized		moody	
efficient		punctual	
forgetful		reliable	
generous		short-tempered	
hardworking		strict	

disorganized

hardworking

B **PAIR WORK** Tell your partner about people you know with these personality traits.

"My boss is very short-tempered. She often shouts at people . . ."

C Listen to four conversations. Then check (✓) the adjective that best describes each person.

1. a boss
   - ☐ creative
   - ☐ forgetful
   - ☐ serious

2. a co-worker
   - ☐ unfriendly
   - ☐ generous
   - ☐ strange

3. a teacher
   - ☐ moody
   - ☐ patient
   - ☐ hardworking

4. a relative
   - ☐ short-tempered
   - ☐ disorganized
   - ☐ reliable

9 PERSPECTIVES Making the right choice

A Listen to these people answer the question, "What kind of work would you like to do?" What job does each person talk about? Do they want that job?

Paula: "Well, I think I'd make a good journalist because I'm good at writing. When I was in high school, I worked as a reporter for the school website. I really enjoyed writing different kinds of articles."

Shawn: "I know what I *don't* want to do! A lot of my friends work in the stock market, but I could never be a stockbroker because I can't make decisions quickly. I don't mind working hard, but I'm terrible under pressure!"

Dalia: "I'm still in school. My parents want me to be a teacher, but I'm not sure yet. I guess I could be a teacher because I'm very creative. I'm also very impatient, so maybe I shouldn't work with kids."

B **PAIR WORK** Look at the interviews again. Who are you most like? least like? Why?

I like working with people. 67

10 GRAMMAR FOCUS

▶ Clauses with *because*

The word *because* introduces a cause or reason.
I'd make a good journalist **because I'm good at writing**.
I could be a teacher **because I'm very creative**.
I wouldn't want to be a teacher **because I'm very impatient**.
I could never be a stockbroker **because I can't make decisions quickly**.

GRAMMAR PLUS see page 141

A Complete the sentences in column A with appropriate information from column B. Then compare with a partner.

A
1. I'd like to be a physical therapist ___
2. I would make a bad librarian ___
3. I couldn't be a diplomat ___
4. I wouldn't mind working as a veterinarian ___
5. I could be a flight attendant ___
6. I could never be a financial advisor ___

B
a. because I'm very disorganized.
b. because I love animals.
c. because I enjoy helping people.
d. because I'm not good at managing money.
e. because I'm short-tempered.
f. because I really enjoy traveling.

B GROUP WORK Think about your personal qualities and skills. Then complete these statements. Take turns discussing them with your group.

I could never be a . . . because . . .
I wouldn't mind working as a . . . because . . .
I'd make a good . . . because . . .
The best job for me is . . . because . . .

11 WRITING An online cover letter for a job application

A Imagine you are applying for one of the jobs in this unit. Write a short cover letter for a job application.

To: Catherine West
Subject: News reporter position – ref. 04532

Reply Forward

Dear Ms. West,
I was excited to see your opening for a news reporter, and I hope to be invited for an interview. I think I could make a great addition to your team because I'm very hardworking, and I really enjoy writing.

As you can see from my résumé, I've had a lot of experience writing for my high school newspaper and for my college website. I also worked . . .

B PAIR WORK Exchange papers. If you received this cover letter, would you invite the applicant for a job interview? Why or why not?

12 READING

A Skim the advertisement. Which three cross-cultural problems does it mention?

GLOBAL WORK SOLUTIONS

At GW Solutions, we recognize the importance of cross-cultural training for U.S. employees working abroad. Lack of cultural understanding results in lost contracts and less business. Here are some examples of what our courses can teach you.

In the U.S.A., we say that time is money. For American workers, punctuality and timetables are always important. At work, people concentrate on the task they are doing. They usually do not spend a lot of time on small talk. However, it's important to realize that not all cultures see time in this way. In many African countries, for example, getting work done isn't the only valuable use of time. Spending time at work to build close relationships with colleagues is equally important. It's important to ask about your colleague's personal life. Understanding these cultural differences is essential for working in a global team. If an American doesn't realize this, he or she might think that an African colleague who spends a lot of time chatting with co-workers is being lazy or avoiding doing his or her work. And an African worker might think their American colleague is the rudest person they've ever met!

In the U.S.A., written agreements are essential. Business deals are always agreed through a contract and once it has been signed, we consider it to be final. The conditions of the agreement don't usually change without the signing of another contract. But you may do business in places where this is not the case. In China, for example, people generally place more trust in a person's word than in a signed contract. Once a good relationship exists, a simple handshake might be enough to reach a business deal.

In the U.S.A., workers generally speak directly, and they openly disagree with colleagues. This kind of "straight talk" is seen as a mark of honesty. But where we see honesty, others may see rudeness. In some parts of Asia, open disagreement with colleagues may not be acceptable because it makes people feel embarrassed. Instead, you should stop and think for a while. Afterward you could say, "I agree in general, but could a different idea work in this situation?" And your body language is important, too. In the West, direct eye contact is good because it's a sign of honesty. In some Asian cultures, it's polite to avoid looking directly at your colleagues in order to show respect.

Did you learn something new? Need to know more? Sign up for one of our training courses and learn how to do business wherever you go.

B Read the advertisement. Then correct the sentences.

1. Ideas about work time are the same in Africa and the U.S.A.
2. Written contracts are more important in China than in the U.S.A.
3. American and Asian workers have similar ways of communicating.

C Complete these sentences with words from the advertisement.

1. In the U.S.A., being _____ is very important at work.
2. African workers like to have strong _____ with their co-workers.
3. In China, people might agree to a business deal with a _____.
4. For Americans, it's normal to _____ openly when they have a different opinion.
5. Some workers _____ making eye contact when talking to others.

D Look at the sentences in part C. Are they true for your country? What advice would you give to a foreigner coming to work in your country?

I like working with people.

Units 9–10 Progress check

SELF-ASSESSMENT

How well can you do these things? Check (✓) the boxes.

I can . . .	Very well	OK	A little
Describe people and things in the past, present, and future (Ex. 1)	☐	☐	☐
Discuss possible consequences of actions (Ex. 2)	☐	☐	☐
Understand descriptions of skills and personality traits (Ex. 3, 4)	☐	☐	☐
Discuss job skills (Ex. 4)	☐	☐	☐
Give reasons for my opinions (Ex. 4)	☐	☐	☐

1 SPEAKING Things have changed.

A PAIR WORK Think of one more question for each category. Then interview a partner.

Free time How did you spend your free time as a child? What do you like to do these days? How are you going to spend your free time next year?

Friends Who used to be your friends when you were a kid? How do you meet new people nowadays? How do you think people will meet in the future?

B GROUP WORK Share one interesting thing about your partner.

2 GAME Share the consequences

A Add two situations and two consequences to the lists below.

Situation
- ☐ you spend too much time online
- ☐ you get a well-paid job
- ☐ you move to a foreign country
- ☐ it's sunny tomorrow
- ☐ you don't study hard
- ☐ you fall in love
- ☐ _____
- ☐ _____

Consequences
- ☐ learn about a different culture
- ☐ get good grades
- ☐ buy an expensive car
- ☐ feel jealous sometimes
- ☐ go to the beach
- ☐ have time for your family and friends
- ☐ _____
- ☐ _____

B CLASS ACTIVITY Go around the class and make sentences. Check (✓) each *if* clause after you use it. The student who uses the most clauses correctly wins.

"If you spend too much time online, you won't . . ."

3 LISTENING What do you want to do?

A Listen to Michelle and Robbie discuss four jobs. Write down the jobs and check (✓) if they would be good or bad at them.

	Job	Good	Bad	Reason
1. Michelle	_____	☐	☐	_____
	_____	☐	☐	_____
2. Robbie	_____	☐	☐	_____
	_____	☐	☐	_____

B Listen again. Write down the reasons they give.

C PAIR WORK Look at the jobs from part A. Which ones would you be good at? Why?

4 DISCUSSION Job profile

A Prepare a personal job profile. Write your name, skills, and job preferences. Think about the questions below. Then compare with a partner.

Do you . . . ?
enjoy helping people
have any special skills
have any experience
have a good memory

Are you good at . . . ?
communicating with people
solving problems
making decisions quickly
learning foreign languages

Do you mind . . . ?
wearing a uniform
traveling frequently
working with a team
working long hours

A: Do you enjoy helping people?
B: Sure. I often do volunteer work.
A: So do I. I help at our local . . .

B GROUP WORK Make suggestions for possible jobs based on your classmates' job profiles. Give reasons for your opinions. What do you think of their suggestions for you?

A: Victor would be a good psychologist because he's good at communicating with people.
B: No way! I could never be a psychologist. I'm very moody and short-tempered!

WHAT'S NEXT?

Look at your Self-assessment again. Do you need to review anything?

11 It's really worth seeing!

▸ Discuss famous landmarks, monuments, and works of art
▸ Discuss countries around the world

1 SNAPSHOT

AMAZING FACTS ABOUT AMAZING LANDMARKS

Machu Picchu – It is located 2,430 m (7,972 ft) above sea level, and it has resisted several earthquakes. When there is an earthquake, the stones "dance" and fall back into place.

The Eiffel Tower – When it was opened in 1889, the tower was red. After a decade, it was painted yellow, and later, it was covered in different shades of brown.

Mount Fuji – The highest mountain in Japan is made up of a few volcanoes. The last recorded eruption started in 1707.

The Neuschwanstein Castle – This beautiful castle in Germany was the inspiration for the Walt Disney Magic Kingdom Sleeping Beauty Castle.

Big Ben – The tower is named Elizabeth Tower. Big Ben is the name of the bell inside it.

The Statue of Liberty – The 350 pieces were made in France and then shipped to the United States.

Did you know these facts about the landmarks above? What else do you know about them?
Have you ever visited any of them? Which would you like to visit? Why?
Do you know any interesting facts about landmarks in your country?

2 PERSPECTIVES Where dreams come true

A How much do you know about the Walt Disney Company and theme parks?
Find three mistakes in the statements below. Then listen and check your answers.

1. The Walt Disney Company was founded in 1923 in California by Walt Disney and his brother Roy.
2. Their most famous character, Donald Duck, first appeared in a movie in 1928.
3. The first Disney theme park, Disneyland, was opened in 1955 in New York and soon became an international attraction.
4. The official opening was broadcast live by the ABC television network.
5. In 1971, the company opened their second park, Disney World.
6. Some of their most popular parks in Florida include Magic Kingdom, Animal Kingdom, and Epcot Center.
7. In 1983, the company opened their first foreign park, London Disneyland. Later, theme parks were also opened in Paris, Hong Kong, and Shanghai.

B GROUP WORK Have you been to a Disney park? Which one?
How did you like it? Which one would you like to go to? Why?

3 GRAMMAR FOCUS

> **Passive with *by* (simple past)**
>
> The passive changes the focus of a sentence.
> For the simple past, use the past of *be* + past participle.
>
> | Active | Passive |
> |---|---|
> | The Disney brothers **founded** the company in 1923. | It **was founded by** the Disney brothers in 1923. |
> | Walt Disney **opened** Disneyland in 1955. | Disneyland **was opened by** Walt Disney in 1955. |
> | The ABC network **broadcast** the opening of the park. | The opening **was broadcast by** ABC. |
>
> **GRAMMAR PLUS** see page 142

A Complete the sentences with the simple past passive form of the verbs. Then compare with a partner.

1. *Mont Sainte-Victoire* _____ (paint) by the French artist Paul Cézanne.
2. The first Star Wars film _____ (write) and _____ (direct) by George Lucas.
3. The Statue of Liberty _____ (design) by the French sculptor Frédéric Auguste Bartholdi.
4. The 2014 World Cup final _____ (win) by Germany. The final match _____ (see) by almost 1 billion people all over the world.
5. The songs *Revolution* and *Hey Jude* _____ (record) by the Beatles in 1968.
6. In the 2007 film *I'm Not There*, the American musician Bob Dylan _____ (play) by six different people, including Australian actress Cate Blanchett.
7. The 2016 Oscar for Best Actress _____ (give) to Brie Larson for her role in the movie *Room*.
8. The first iPad _____ (release) in 2010.

B **PAIR WORK** Change these sentences into passive sentences with *by*.
Then take turns reading them aloud.

1. Eddie Redmayne played Stephen Hawking in the 2014 film *The Theory of Everything*.
   _____
2. Gabriel García Márquez wrote the novel *One Hundred Years of Solitude* in 1967.
   _____
3. The American architect William Lamb designed the Empire State Building.
   _____
4. Woo Paik produced the first digital HDTV in 1991.
   _____
5. J. K. Rowling wrote the first Harry Potter book on an old manual typewriter.
   _____
6. *Empire* magazine readers chose Indiana Jones as the greatest movie character of all time.
   _____

4 INTERCHANGE 11 True or false?

Who created these well-known works? Go to Interchange 11 on page 125.

It's really worth seeing! **73**

5 PRONUNCIATION The letter o

A Listen and practice. Notice how the letter o is pronounced in the following words.

/a/	/ou/	/u/	/ʌ/
not	no	do	one
top	don't	food	love
___	___	___	___
___	___	___	___

B How is the letter o pronounced in these words? Write them in the correct column in part A. Then listen and check your answers.

come   done   lock   own   shot   soon   who   wrote

6 LISTENING Man-made wonders of the world

A Listen to three tour guides describe some famous monuments. Take notes to answer the questions below. Then compare with a partner.

1. Taj Mahal
Why was it built?
What do the changing colors of the building represent?

2. Palace of Versailles
What did King Louis XIV want the Hall of Mirrors to show?
What problem did the candles cause? How did the mirrors help?

3. La Sagrada Familia
What did the architect think about man-made structures versus nature?
Why are no straight lines used?

B PAIR WORK Think of another famous monument. Describe it to the rest of the class. They will try to guess the monument.

7 WORD POWER Country fast facts

A Complete the sentences with words from the list.

✓ cattle	dialects	electronics	handicrafts	languages
sheep	souvenirs	✓ soybeans	textiles	wheat

1. The United States **grows** __soybeans__ and _____.
2. Australia **raises** __cattle__ and _____.
3. China **manufactures** _____ and _____.
4. In India, people **speak** many different _____ and _____.
5. You can **find** _____ and _____ at different shops in Brazil.

B PAIR WORK Talk about your country. Use the sentences in part A with your own information.

"We raise cattle and chickens. We grow corn and oats. You can find . . ."

8 CONVERSATION What do you want to know?

A Listen and practice.

Lisa: Erik, you're from Amsterdam, aren't you?
Erik: Yeah . . . Why?
Lisa: I'm going there for a conference, and I'd like some information.
Erik: Sure. What do you want to know?
Lisa: Do you use the euro in the Netherlands?
Erik: Yes. The euro is used in most of Europe, you know.
Lisa: And do I need to take euros with me?
Erik: Not really. International credit cards are accepted everywhere, and they're much safer.
Lisa: Of course. And what should I buy there?
Erik: Cheese, definitely. We raise dairy cows, and some really excellent cheese is made from their milk.
Lisa: Good. I love cheese. Where is it sold?
Erik: You can find it at cheese shops all around the city. And don't forget to bring me a piece.

B Listen to the rest of the conversation. What other suggestion does Erik give Lisa?

9 GRAMMAR FOCUS

Passive without *by* (simple present)

For the simple present, use the present of *be* + past participle.

Active	Passive
They **use** the euro in most of Europe.	The euro **is used** in most of Europe.
Most places **accept** credit cards.	Credit cards **are accepted** at most places.
We **raise** dairy cattle in the Netherlands.	Dairy cattle **are raised** in the Netherlands.

GRAMMAR PLUS see page 142

A Complete the sentences. Use the passive of these verbs.

| grow | manufacture | raise | speak | sell | use |

1. French and Flemish _____ in Belgium.
2. Rice _____ in many Asian countries.
3. Cars and electronics _____ in Japan.
4. Sheep's milk _____ for making feta cheese.
5. Handicrafts _____ in the streets in Thailand.
6. A lot of cattle _____ in Australia.

B Complete this passage using the simple present passive form.

Many crops _____ (grow) in Taiwan. Some crops _____ (consume) locally, but others _____ (export). Tea _____ (grow) in cooler parts of the island, and rice _____ (cultivate) in warmer parts. Fishing is also an important industry. A wide variety of seafood _____ (catch) and _____ (ship) all over the world. Many people _____ (employ) in the food-processing industry.

C PAIR WORK Use the passive of the verbs in part A to talk about your country and other countries you know.

It's really worth seeing! 75

10 LISTENING Is all tourism good?

A Listen to a news report about tourism in Costa Rica. Select the six effects of mass tourism that are mentioned. (There are two extra effects.) Indicate if they are positive (**P**) or negative (**N**).

P	English is spoken.		The ocean is polluted.
	Tourism jobs are available all over the country.		High-rise hotels are built.
	More foreigners are investing there.		Fish and lobster are hunted.
	Acres of jungle are cut down.		The government becomes corrupt.

Costa Rica

B Listen again. Write down three criteria the hotel fulfills in order to be an ecotourism business in Costa Rica.

_____   _____   _____

C **GROUP WORK** What is tourism like in your country? Talk about some positive and negative aspects.

11 SPEAKING Give me a clue.

A **PAIR WORK** Choose a country. Then answer these questions.

Where is it located?
What traditional dishes are eaten there?
What languages are spoken?
What currency is used?
What famous tourist attraction is found there?
What souvenirs are found there?

B **CLASS ACTIVITY** Give a short talk about the country you chose. Don't say the country's name. Can the class guess the country?

12 WRITING A city guide

A Choose a city or area in your country and write the introduction for an online city guide. Include the location, size, population, main attractions, shopping and travel tips, etc.

> Bruges is located in the northwest of Belgium, and it has a population of about 120,000 people. It is known for its canals and medieval buildings. In 2000, it was declared a World Heritage City by UNESCO. Bruges is also a good place to buy Belgium chocolate. It is sold …

Bruges, Belgium

B **GROUP WORK** Exchange papers. Do you think the introduction gives a good idea of the place? Would it attract tourists or businesses to the place? What other information should be included?

13 READING

A Scan the advertisements. How many types of toilets can you see at the museum? When were the underwater sculptures designed? How big is the world's smallest book?

A SULABH INTERNATIONAL MUSEUM OF TOILETS, NEW DELHI, INDIA

Ever wondered about the history of toilets? Probably not! But visit the fascinating Sulabh Museum and see just how interesting they can be. Admire nearly 300 different toilets dating back to 2500 B.C.E. Some are beautifully decorated, one is made of solid gold, and there is an electric toilet that works without water. The star of the collection is a copy of a 16th century toilet. It was used by King Louis XIV of France – sometimes while speaking to his government. See drawings, photographs, and poems about toilets, too. One photo shows a toilet that was used by an elephant!

B UNDERWATER MUSEUM, CANCUN, MEXICO

Join one of our unique tours and discover an amazing underwater world 27 feet below the sea. Designed by Jason deCaires Taylor in 2009, it has over 450 sculptures. They are made from natural materials and show art and nature existing side by side. The *Silent Evolution* shows men, women, and children standing together on the seabed. They look so real that you'll want to talk to them. There are also sculptures of a house and a life-size Beetle car. The sculptures are covered in beautiful corals, and their appearances are constantly changing. Watch as an incredible variety of fish swim in and out of them.

C MICROMINIATURE MUSEUM, KIEV, UKRAINE

Small really is beautiful in this museum of art with a difference. The exhibits, created by artist Nikolai Syadristy, are so tiny they can only be seen clearly with a microscope. Read the world's smallest book – it is only 0.6 millimeters in size, but contains twelve pages of poems and drawings. There is a chess set on the head of a pin and the world's smallest electric motor. It is 20 times smaller than a piece of sand. Look closely at the eye of a needle and discover the seven camels inside. Read the words "Long Live Peace" not on paper, but written on a human hair!

B Read the advertisements. Find the words in *italics* below. Then circle the meaning of each word.
1. Something *fascinating* makes you feel very **interested / angry**.
2. The *star* of a collection is the **worst / best** part.
3. A *unique* thing is **different from / the same as** all others.
4. If something is changing *constantly*, it's changing **very little / all the time**.
5. An *exhibit* is an object that is **on show / for sale**.
6. A *needle* is a metal object that is used for **cutting / sewing**.

C Read the comments of three visitors to the museums. Write the letter (A, B, or C) of the museum you think they visited.
_____ 1. "I just don't know how he made such little things."
_____ 2. "I can't believe that an animal would use something like that."
_____ 3. "I felt a little afraid about going down, but it was a great experience in the end."

D Which museum would you most like to visit? Why?

It's really worth seeing!

12 It's a long story.

▶ Tell stories
▶ Discuss recent activities

1 SNAPSHOT

True Stories of Incredible Coincidences

One day, the American novelist Anne Parrish was in a bookstore in Paris and she saw an old, used copy of one of her favorite childhood books. When she opened it, she saw on the first page: "Anne Parrish, 209 N. Weber Street, Colorado Springs." It was Anne's own book.

A 10-year-old girl named Laura Buxton released a bunch of balloons into the air. She attached a note to the balloons that asked the person who found it to write back to her. A couple of weeks later, she received a reply. It was from another 10-year-old girl also named Laura Buxton who lived 150 miles away.

Which of these stories do you think is more amazing? more difficult to believe?
Have you ever had an experience that is hard to believe?
Do you know of anyone who has? What happened?

2 PERSPECTIVES What next?

A Listen to what happened to these people. Check (✓) the things that have happened to you.

- ☐ "I was having lunch when I spilled a cup of coffee on my clothes."
- ☐ "I was driving to the airport to pick up a friend, but I got a flat tire."
- ☐ "I was studying for an important test when the lights went out."
- ☐ "While I was walking down the street, I found a wallet with lots of money."
- ☐ "I was traveling in another country when I met an old school friend."
- ☐ "I was getting off a bus when I slipped and fell on the sidewalk."
- ☐ "While I was shopping one day, a celebrity walked into the store."

B Choose one statement that you checked. What happened next?

"I tried to clean it, but I couldn't. So I had to wear a jacket for the rest of the day."

3 GRAMMAR FOCUS

Past continuous vs. simple past

Use the past continuous for an action in progress in the past.
Use the simple past for an action that interrupts it.

I **was having** lunch	when I **spilled** coffee on my clothes.
I **was driving** to the airport,	but I **got** a flat tire.
While I **was shopping** one day,	a celebrity **walked** into the store.

GRAMMAR PLUS see page 143

A Complete these sentences. Then compare with a partner.

1. My sister _____ (text) while she _____ (drive), and she almost _____ (crash) her car.
2. While I _____ (cook) dinner last night, a friend _____ (call) and I _____ (burn) the food.
3. My father _____ (ski) when he _____ (break) his leg in several places.
4. We _____ (have) our first child while we _____ (live) in a tiny apartment.
5. While I _____ (drive) in England a few years ago, I _____ (realize) I was on the wrong side of the road!
6. Once I _____ (read) a good book, but someone _____ (tell) me the ending.
7. My parents _____ (meet) each other while they _____ (work) at the same restaurant in Vancouver.

B Complete these statements with information about yourself. Use the simple past or the past continuous.

1. I was taking a selfie when . . .
2. While I was going home one day, . . .
3. I was . . .
4. While I was . . .
5. Last month, . . .
6. Some time ago, . . .

C **PAIR WORK** Take turns reading your sentences from part B. Then ask and answer follow-up questions.

A: I was taking a selfie when a man came and stole my phone.
B: Oh, no! What did you do?
A: I went to the police . . . and they told me to be more careful.

It's a long story.

4 LISTENING How did it all begin?

A Listen to this story about a successful inventor. Put the sentences into the correct order from 1 to 8.

_1_ Mark Zuckerberg started writing computer programs.
___ His friends invested in Facebook.
___ He didn't accept Microsoft's offer.
___ He invented FaceMash.
___ Facebook became available to the public.
___ Zuckerberg wrote his very own messenger program.
___ He created a program that recommended music.
___ Three classmates asked for his help.

B Listen again. How did the invention change his life?

C PAIR WORK Think of other websites and apps that were successful inventions.

5 WORD POWER What happened?

A Some adverbs are often used in storytelling to emphasize that something interesting is about to happen. Which of these adverbs are positive (**P**)? Which are negative (**N**)? Which could be either (**E**)?

coincidentally	___	strangely	___
fortunately	___	suddenly	___
luckily	___	surprisingly	___
miraculously	___	unexpectedly	___
sadly	___	unfortunately	___

B PAIR WORK Complete these statements with adverbs from part A to make up creative sentences.

We were having a party when, . . .
I was walking down the street when, . . .
It started out as a normal day, but, . . .

A: We were having a party when, suddenly, the lights went out!
B: Once I was dancing at a party when, unfortunately, I fell down!

6 WRITING What's your story?

A Write a short story about something that happened to you recently. Try to include some of the adverbs from Exercise 5.

> I was shopping at a big department store when, suddenly, I saw a little girl crying in a corner all by herself. The girl said she couldn't find her mother. I was taking her to the store manager when I saw an old school friend running towards me. Coincidentally, she was the girl's mother, and . . .

B GROUP WORK Take turns reading your stories. Answer any questions from the group.

7 CONVERSATION What have you been doing?

A Listen and practice.

Steve: Hey, Luiza! I haven't seen you in ages. What have you been doing lately?
Luiza: I haven't been going out much. I've been working two jobs for the last six months.
Steve: How come?
Luiza: I'm saving up money for a trip to Morocco.
Steve: Well, that's exciting!
Luiza: Yeah, it is. What about you?
Steve: Well, I've only been *spending* money. I've been trying to become an actor. I've been taking courses and going to a lot of auditions.
Luiza: Really? How long have you been trying?
Steve: Since I graduated. But I haven't had any luck yet. No one recognizes my talent.

B Listen to two other people at the party. What has happened since they last saw each other?

8 GRAMMAR FOCUS

Present perfect continuous

Use the present perfect continuous for actions that start in the past and continue into the present.

What **have** you **been doing** lately?   I**'ve been working** two jobs for the last six months.
How long **have** you **been trying**?   I**'ve been trying** since I graduated.
Have you **been saving** money?   No, I **haven't been saving** money. I**'ve been spending** it!

GRAMMAR PLUS see page 143

A Complete the conversations with the present perfect continuous.

1. **A:** _____ you _____ (learn) any new skills this year?
   B: Yes, I have. I _____ (take) some art courses.
2. **A:** What _____ you _____ (do) lately?
   B: Well, I _____ (look for) a new job.
3. **A:** How _____ you _____ (feel) recently?
   B: Great! I _____ (run) three times a week. And I _____ (not drink) as much coffee since I stopped working at the coffee shop.
4. **A:** _____ you _____ (get) enough exercise lately?
   B: No, I haven't. I _____ (study) a lot for a big exam.

B PAIR WORK Read the conversations in part A together. Then read them again and answer the questions with your own information.

A: Have you been learning any new skills this year?
B: Yes, I've been taking guitar lessons.

It's a long story.   **81**

9 PRONUNCIATION Contrastive stress in responses

A Listen and practice. Notice how the stress changes to emphasize a contrast.

A: Has your brother been studying German?
B: No, **I've** been studying German.

A: Have you been teaching French?
B: No, I've been **studying** French.

B Mark the stress changes in these conversations. Listen and check. Then practice the conversations.

A: Have you been studying for ten years?
B: No, I've been studying for two years.

A: Have you been studying at school?
B: No, I've been studying at home.

10 SPEAKING Tell me about it.

GROUP WORK Add three questions to this list. Then take turns asking and answering the questions. Remember to ask for further information.

Have you been . . . lately?

traveling
watching any good TV series
taking any lessons
working out
working long hours
going out a lot
staying up late

_____
_____
_____

useful expressions

Really?
I didn't know that!
Oh, I see.
I had no idea.
Wow! Tell me more.

A: Have you been traveling lately?
B: Yes, I have. I've been going abroad about once a month.
C: Really? Lucky you!
B: Not exactly. I've been traveling for work, not on vacation.

11 INTERCHANGE 12 It's my life.

Play a board game. Go to Interchange 12 on page 126.

12 READING

A Skim the article. What is special about these musicians? How have they influenced other people?

BREAKING DOWN THE SOUND OF SILENCE

Ten years before he died, the composer Beethoven went deaf. He called this disability his "nightmare." Fortunately for thousands of classical music fans, he didn't stop writing brilliant music. One hundred and eighty years later, being deaf hasn't stopped three Americans – Steve Longo, Ed Chevy, and Bob Hiltermann – from playing music, either. In their case, the music is rock, and their band is called Beethoven's Nightmare.

The three boys grew up in different cities, but they all showed a surprising interest in music. Although they couldn't hear it, they were amazed by the energy of 1960s bands like the Beatles. They could see the effect the music had on the audiences – the happy faces of friends and family as they watched. Something exciting was obviously happening. "I'm going to do that, too," they all said. "Why? You can't hear," asked parents, teachers, and friends alike. Each boy used sign language to answer, "Because I can feel it."

Longo and Chevy started playing the guitar. They put on headphones and turned up the volume. With the help of powerful hearing aids, they could get some of the notes – the rest they felt through vibrations. Drummer Hiltermann came from a musical family. His parents thought that teaching their son to play an instrument was a waste of time. But they changed their minds after he nearly drove them crazy by using knives and forks to drum on the furniture of the house.

The three men first met in college in Washington, D.C. They started a band and played many concerts until they graduated in 1975. In 2001, Hiltermann had the idea to bring his old friends together again. They have been performing ever since. In 2013, a new member, Paul Raci, joined the band as a singer. At concerts, dancers put on a spectacular show and use sign language to explain the words of the songs to the audience. And, of course, the band plays very loudly!

The group has encouraged many deaf people, and people with other disabilities, to follow their dreams. Chevy says, "The only thing deaf people *can't* do is hear."

Dennis McCarthy, "Deaf band 'Beethoven's Nightmare' feels the music," *Los Angeles Daily News* (Oct. 31, 2013). Used with permission.

B Read the article. Choose the correct word(s) in the sentences below.
1. After going deaf, Beethoven **continued / refused** to compose music.
2. The boys knew music was powerful because of something they **read / saw**.
3. Many people didn't **understand / like** the boys' ambition to play music.
4. Hiltermann's parents **wanted / didn't want** him to learn to play at first.
5. The three young men started playing together **before / after** finishing college.

C Answer the questions.
1. Which band inspired the three boys to play music?
2. What did Longo and Chevy use to hear some parts of the music?
3. What did Hiltermann use to make noise in his house?
4. Where did the three men get to know each other?
5. When did Beethoven's Nightmare start playing?

D Do you think it's very difficult for people in your country to achieve their dreams? What new technology and facilities make it easier for them?

It's a long story.

Units 11–12 Progress check

SELF-ASSESSMENT

How well can you do these things? Check (✓) the boxes.

I can . . .	Very well	OK	A little
Give information about books, movies, songs, etc. (Ex. 1)	☐	☐	☐
Understand information about countries (Ex. 2)	☐	☐	☐
Describe a situation (Ex. 3)	☐	☐	☐
Ask and answer questions about past events (Ex. 4, 5)	☐	☐	☐
Ask and answer questions about recent activities (Ex. 5)	☐	☐	☐

1 SPEAKING Trivia questions

A List six books, movies, songs, albums, or other popular works. Then write one *who* question for each of the six items.

> Harry Potter books
> Who wrote the Harry Potter books?

B PAIR WORK Take turns asking your questions. Use the passive with *by* to answer.

A: Who wrote the *Harry Potter* books?
B: I think they were written by J. K. Rowling.

2 LISTENING Did you know?

A Listen to a game show about Spain. Write the correct answers.

1. How many languages are officially recognized? _____
2. What day is considered bad luck? _____
3. What is the most valuable soccer team in the world? _____
4. In how many countries is Spanish the official language? _____
5. What fruit is thrown at the world's biggest food fight? _____
6. What is Spain's famous dance called? _____

B Listen again. Keep score. How much money does each contestant have?

3 GAME What happened?

GROUP WORK Use the passive to write details about these situations. Then compare with the class. Which group wrote the most sentences?

The lights went out.
Our class was canceled.

It snowed a lot yesterday.
Many roads were blocked.

Your roommate cleaned the apartment.
The dishes were done.

4 ROLE PLAY Do you have an alibi?

> A famous painting has been stolen from a local museum. It disappeared last Sunday afternoon between 12:00 P.M. and 4:00 P.M.

Student A: Student B suspects you stole the painting. Make up an alibi. Take notes on what you were doing that day. Then answer Student B's questions.

Student B: You are a police detective. You think Student A stole the painting. Add two questions to the notebook. Then ask Student A the questions.

Where were you last Sunday?
Where did you go for lunch?
Did anyone see you?
What were you wearing that day?
What were you doing between noon and 4:00 P.M.?
Was anyone with you?
_____
_____

Change roles and try the role play again.

5 DISCUSSION Is that so?

A GROUP WORK What interesting things can you find out about your classmates? Ask these questions and others of your own.

Have you been doing anything exciting recently?
Where do you live? How long have you been living there?
Have you met anyone interesting lately?
Who is your best friend? How did you meet? How long have you been friends?
Where were you living ten years ago? Did you like it there? What do you remember about it?

useful expressions

Really?
I didn't know that!
Oh, I see.
I had no idea.
Wow! Tell me more.

B CLASS ACTIVITY Tell the class the most interesting thing you learned.

WHAT'S NEXT?

Look at your Self-assessment again. Do you need to review anything?

13 That's entertainment!

- Discuss popular entertainment
- Discuss movies and famous Hollywood names

1 SNAPSHOT

MOVIE TRIVIA

Black Mass (2015) Sienna Miller spent months rehearsing and filming, but in the end, the director decided to cut out all her scenes for "narrative reasons."

Django Unchained (2012) In the movie, Leonardo DiCaprio was supposed to slam a table, but accidentally slammed a glass and cut his hand. The scene was so good that the director decided to incorporate it.

Furious 7 (2015) Actor Paul Walker died while still shooting the movie. The director used computer technology and stunts to finish the remaining scenes.

Avatar (2009) The special effects were so expensive that director James Cameron had to wait 10 years to make the movie.

The Princess and the Frog (2009) After watching the movie, about fifty children got sick with salmonella from kissing frogs.

Paranormal Activity (2007) This movie only cost $15,000 to make, but it made $9.1 million in its first week.

Which of the movie trivia do you find most interesting?
Do you know any other movie trivia?
Which of these movies have you seen? Did you enjoy it? Which would you like to watch?

2 CONVERSATION I think they're boring.

A Listen and practice.

Danny: It's so hot out. Do you want to stay in and watch a movie this afternoon?
Gina: Hmm. Maybe. What do you want to see?
Danny: How about an *X-Men* movie? I've heard that the early ones are really interesting.
Gina: For you, maybe. I'm not interested in action movies. Actually, I think they're boring.
Danny: What about that new movie based on one of Stephen King's novels?
Gina: I don't know. I'm always fascinated by his books, but I'm not in the mood for a horror movie.
Danny: Well, what do you want to see?
Gina: How about a *Game of Thrones* marathon? It's my favorite series ever.
Danny: OK, but only if you make us some popcorn.

B Listen to the rest of the conversation. What happens next? What do they decide to do?

3 GRAMMAR FOCUS

Participles as adjectives

Present participles
That *X-Men* movie sounds **interesting**.
Stephen King's books are **fascinating**.
I think action movies are **boring**.

Past participles
I'm not **interested** in action movies.
I'm **fascinated** by Stephen King's books.
I'm **bored** by action movies.

GRAMMAR PLUS see page 144

A Complete these sentences. Then compare with a partner.

1. John Cho is such an _____ actor. I'm always _____ by his incredible talent. (amaze)
2. Most TV shows are really _____. I often get so _____ watching them that I fall asleep. (bore)
3. I was _____ in watching *The Martian* after I read the book. And I was surprised that the movie is really _____. (interest)
4. I'm _____ to watch *The Avengers*. Everybody has told me it's really _____. (excite)
5. I find animated films very _____. I've been _____ by them since I was a little kid. (amuse / fascinate)
6. It's _____ that horror movies are so popular. I can't understand why people go to the movies to feel _____. (surprise / terrify)

John Cho

B **PAIR WORK** Complete the description below with the correct forms of the words.

amaze   annoy   confuse   disgust   embarrass   shock

I had a terrible time at the movies last weekend. First, my ticket cost $25. I was really _____ by the price. By mistake, I gave the cashier two $5 bills instead of a twenty and a five. I was a little _____. Then there was trash all over the theater. The mess was _____. The people behind me were talking during the movie, which was _____. The story was hard to follow. I always find thrillers so _____. I liked the special effects, though. They were _____!

4 WORD POWER How do you like it?

A **PAIR WORK** Complete the chart with synonyms from the list.

amusing	dumb	horrible	odd	silly
bizarre	fantastic	hysterical	outstanding	terrible
disgusting	hilarious	incredible	ridiculous	weird

Awful	Wonderful	Stupid	Strange	Funny

B **GROUP WORK** Share your opinions about a movie, an actor, an actress, a TV show, and a book. Use words from part A.

That's entertainment!

5 LISTENING What did you think?

A Listen to people talk about books, movies, and TV programs. Match each conversation to the statement that best describes the people's opinions.

1. ___   a. This special offers an amazing look into an exotic country.
2. ___   b. The new investigation into these creatures was a waste of time.
3. ___   c. The bad acting with this boring idea makes it terrible.
4. ___   d. She is excited to read more of this clever mystery series.

B Listen again. Write a reason each person gives to support his or her opinion.

1. _____   3. _____
2. _____   4. _____

6 PRONUNCIATION Emphatic stress

A Listen and practice. Notice how stress and a higher pitch are used to express strong opinions.

That was terrible!   He was amazing!   That's fascinating!

B PAIR WORK Write four statements using these words. Then take turns reading them. Pay attention to emphatic stress.

fantastic   horrible   ridiculous   weird

7 DISCUSSION I give it two thumbs up!

A PAIR WORK Take turns asking and answering these questions and others of your own.

What kinds of movies are you interested in? Why?
What kinds of movies do you find boring?
Who are your favorite actors and actresses? Why?
Are there actors or actresses you don't like?
What's the worst movie you've ever seen?
Are there any outstanding movies playing now?
Do you prefer to watch films dubbed or with subtitles? Why?

A: What kinds of movies are you interested in?
B: I like romantic comedies.
A: Really? Why is that?
B: They're entertaining! What about you?
A: I think romantic comedies are kind of dumb. I prefer . . .

B GROUP WORK Compare your information. Whose taste in movies is most like yours?

ACTION
COMEDY
ANIMATION
FANTASY
BIOGRAPHY
SCI-FI
THRILLER
HORROR
DRAMA
WAR
DOCUMENTARY

8 PERSPECTIVES And the Oscar goes to . . .

A Listen to people talk about some of their Hollywood favorites. Can you guess the actress, actor, or movie each person is describing?

1. He's a famous American actor who is also a successful director and producer. He won the Oscar for Best Motion Picture in 2013 with *Argo*, which he directed and co-produced.

2. The first movie in the series came out in 1977. It's a science fiction fantasy that has become a blockbuster franchise. The story takes place "a long time ago in a galaxy far, far away."

3. I really like animated movies, and the third one in this series is my favorite. It's about a boy's toys that have a secret life full of adventures when they are alone.

4. She's an actress that is excellent in both dramas and comedies. I loved her in *Mamma Mia!* and *The Devil Wears Prada*. In 2011, she won her third Oscar for her performance in *The Iron Lady*.

B Do you like the people and movies described in part A? What else do you know about them?

9 GRAMMAR FOCUS

Relative pronouns for people and things

Use *who* or *that* for people.

He's an actor. He's also a director and producer.
He's an actor **who/that** is also a director and producer.

Use *which* or *that* for things.

It's a science fiction fantasy. It has become a blockbuster franchise.
It's a science fiction fantasy **which/that** has become a blockbuster franchise.

GRAMMAR PLUS see page 144

A Combine the sentences using relative pronouns. Then compare with a partner.

1. Jennifer Hudson is a singer. She's acted in several films.
2. *The Phantom of the Opera* is based on a French novel. It was published in 1911.
3. *Spiderman* and *Transformers* are successful franchises. They were adapted from comic books.
4. Michael Keaton is a famous Hollywood actor. He began his career as a cameraman.
5. Dakota Fanning is an actress. She made her first movie when she was only seven years old.
6. Wii Fit is a video game. It helps people to get more exercise.
7. Stephenie Meyer is an American writer. She wrote the *Twilight* series.
8. Many Hollywood stars live in Beverly Hills. It's a small city near Los Angeles, California.

Jennifer Hudson

B PAIR WORK Complete these sentences. Then compare your information around the class.

1. Adele is a singer and songwriter . . .
2. *Fantastic Four* is a movie franchise . . .
3. *The Voice* is a reality show . . .
4. Scarlett Johansson is an actress . . .

10 INTERCHANGE 13 It was hilarious!

How do you like movies and TV shows? Go to Interchange 13 on page 127.

That's entertainment! 89

11 SPEAKING Pilot episode

A PAIR WORK A TV studio is looking for ideas for a new TV show. Brainstorm possible ideas and agree on an idea. Make brief notes.

What kind of TV show is it?
What's it about?
Who are the main characters?
Who is this show for?

B CLASS ACTIVITY Tell the class about your TV show.

"Our TV show is a comedy. It's about two very lazy friends who discover a time machine and travel to the time of the dinosaurs. Then . . ."

12 LISTENING At the movies

A Listen to two critics, Nicole and Anthony, talk about a new movie. Check (✓) the features of the movie that they discuss. (There are two extra features.)

	Nicole's opinion	Anthony's opinion
☐ acting		
☐ story		
☐ writing		
☐ music		
☐ love story		
☐ special effects		

B Listen again. Write Nicole and Anthony's opinions of each feature.

13 WRITING A movie review

A PAIR WORK Choose a movie you both have seen and discuss it. Then write a review of it.

What was the movie about?
What did you like about it?
What didn't you like about it?
How was the acting?
How would you rate it?

B CLASS ACTIVITY Read your review to the class. Who else has seen the movie? Do they agree with your review?

MOVIE TALK LOGIN / REGISTER

We recently streamed *Birdman*, which won the Academy Award for Best Picture in 2015. It's about an actor who made successful movies in Hollywood in the past, and now tries to reinvent his career on Broadway. It stars Michael Keaton and Emma Stone as a father and daughter. We liked the movie because it is both a drama and a comedy. I didn't like . . .

BEST PICTURE
BIRDMAN
OR (THE UNEXPECTED VIRTUE OF IGNORANCE)

14   12

14 READING

A Scan the article. Which movies are mentioned? When were they released?

THE REAL ART OF ACTING

1 Acting can bring fame, money, and success. But it's not always easy. Good acting is not only about learning lines and dressing up. It's also about convincing the audience that you really are somebody else. [a] To achieve this, good actors sometimes put themselves through unpleasant experiences.

2 Actors often have to lose or gain a lot of weight in order to play a part. In *The Machinist* (2005), Christian Bale plays an extremely thin factory worker who suffers from insomnia. [b] Four months before he began filming, Bale started a crazy diet. He only ate an apple and a can of tuna a day and lost 63 pounds. Although he wanted to lose another 20 pounds, the producers persuaded him to stop because they were worried about his health. When filming ended, he had just six months to gain the incredible 100 pounds he needed to play Bruce Wayne in *Batman Begins*. [c]

3 Physical training can also be a challenge. Steven Spielberg wanted to show the real horror of war in *Saving Private Ryan* (1998) and he wanted his actors to feel like real soldiers. So he sent a group of them, including Tom Hanks, to a 10-day military boot camp. [d] They ran miles every day, slept outside in the freezing cold, and were given little food. In the end, all of them were physically and mentally exhausted. Natalie Portman also had to make a great physical effort when she got the role of a ballerina in *Black Swan* (2010). Before filming, she spent a whole year training for eight hours a day, six days a week in order to learn to dance. Once filming began, things didn't get easier either. Portman dislocated a rib while dancing. Nevertheless, she bravely continued filming during the six weeks it took her to recover.

4 Sometimes "becoming" a character can mean saying goodbye to the real world and everybody in it completely. Actor Heath Ledger locked himself in a hotel room for six weeks when he was preparing to play the role of Joker in *The Dark Knight* (2008). He slept only two hours a day and he spent the rest of the time practicing how to walk, talk, and move like his character. [e] It seems he was successful in the end, as audiences and critics loved his work, and he won an Oscar for the part.

B Read the article. Where do these sentences belong? Write a–e.

1. The actors' lives became very hard. ___
2. Not sleeping is making him sick. ___
3. And he didn't speak to anybody at all. ___
4. The character has to be believable. ___
5. So he ate lots of pizza and ice cream. ___

C Find words in the text to match these definitions.

1. The words that actors say in a movie (paragraph 1) _____
2. People who control how a movie is made (paragraph 2) _____
3. A bone in a person's chest (paragraph 3) _____
4. The people who write reviews of movies or books (paragraph 4) _____

D Which of these unpleasant experiences is the worst? Do you think it's necessary for an actor to do this kind of thing for a part?

That's entertainment!

14 Now I get it!

▸ Discuss the meaning of gestures and body language
▸ Discuss rules and recognize common signs

1 SNAPSHOT

POPULAR EMOJIS

- I am not amused.
- I'm laughing so hard, I'm crying!
- I'm bored.
- Great job!
- That's amazing!
- I'm so embarrassed.
- I love it!
- That's awful!
- Just kidding!
- My heart is breaking.

Do you use these emojis? In what situations do you use them?
What other expressions can you use emojis to convey?
What is the weirdest emoji you've ever seen? the funniest? the hardest to understand?

2 WORD POWER Body language

A What is this woman doing in each picture? Match each description with a picture. Then compare with a partner.

1. She's scratching her head. _____
2. She's biting her nails. _____
3. She's rolling her eyes. _____
4. She's tapping her foot. _____
5. She's pulling her hair out. _____
6. She's wrinkling her nose. _____

B **GROUP WORK** Use the pictures in part A and these adjectives to describe how the woman is feeling.

| annoyed | confused | embarrassed | frustrated | irritated |
| bored | disgusted | exhausted | impatient | nervous |

"In the first picture, she's tapping her foot. She looks impatient."

3 CONVERSATION It's pretty confusing.

A Listen and practice.

Eva: How was dinner with the new Bulgarian student last night? What's her name – Elena?

Brian: Yeah, Elena. It was nice. We always have a good time, but I still don't understand her very well. You see, when we offer her something to eat or drink, she nods her head up and down. But, at the same time she says no.

Eva: It might mean she wants to accept it, but she thinks it's not polite. In some countries, you have to refuse any offer first. Then the host insists, and you accept it.

Brian: I don't know . . . It's pretty confusing.

Eva: It could mean she doesn't want anything, but she thinks it's rude to say no.

Jack: Actually, in some countries, when people move their heads up and down, it means "no."

Brian: Really? Now I get it!

B Now listen to Elena talk to her friend. What does she find unusual about the way people in North America communicate?

4 GRAMMAR FOCUS

Modals and adverbs

Modals
It **might/may** mean she wants to accept it.
It **could** mean she doesn't want anything.
That **must** mean "no."

Adverbs
Maybe/Perhaps it means she wants to accept it.
It **probably** means she doesn't want anything.
That **definitely** means "no."

GRAMMAR PLUS see page 145

PAIR WORK What do these gestures mean? Take turns making statements about each gesture. Use the meanings in the box or your own ideas.

possible meanings
I don't know.
Be quiet.
Call me.
That sounds crazy!
I can't hear you.
Come here.

A: What do you think the first gesture means?
B: It probably means . . . , OR It might mean . . .

Now I get it! **93**

5 PRONUNCIATION Pitch

A Listen and practice. Notice how pitch is used to express certainty or doubt.

	Certain	Uncertain
A: Do you think her gesture means "no"?	B: Definitely.	B: Probably.
A: Do you understand what her gesture means?	B: Absolutely.	B: Maybe.

B PAIR WORK Take turns asking yes/no questions. Respond by using *absolutely*, *definitely*, *maybe*, *probably*, and your own information. Pay attention to pitch.

6 SPEAKING What's the matter with me?

A GROUP WORK Imagine you have one of these problems. What could explain it?

- I'm always late for class.
- I'm always exhausted at the end of the day.
- I'm often irritated with everybody at the office.
- I'm always broke.
- I'm often bored.
- I often argue with my friends.

A: I'm always exhausted at the end of the day.
B: It might mean you are not getting enough sleep.
C: It could mean you are working too hard.
D: That definitely means . . .

B CLASS ACTIVITY Who came up with the most interesting explanation in your group? the most unexpected?

7 INTERCHANGE 14 Casual observers

Interpret people's body language. Go to Interchange 14 on page 128.

94 Unit 14

8 PERSPECTIVES Rules and regulations

A What do you think these signs mean? Listen and match each sign with the correct meaning.

1. ___   2. ___   3. ___   4. ___
5. ___   6. ___   7. ___   8. ___

a. You can swim here.
b. You aren't allowed to take photos here.
c. You have to fasten your seat belts.
d. You've got to take off your shoes to enter.
e. You are allowed to park here.
f. You can't turn left.
g. Pets aren't allowed in this area.
h. You have to turn off electronic devices in this area.

B **PAIR WORK** Where might you see the signs in part A? Give two suggestions for each one.

"You might see this one by a lake . . ."

9 GRAMMAR FOCUS

Permission, obligation, and prohibition

Permission
You **can** swim here.
You**'re allowed to** park here.

Obligation
You **have to** fasten your seat belt.
You**'ve got to** take off your shoes.

Prohibition
You **can't** turn left.
Pets **aren't allowed** in this area.

GRAMMAR PLUS see page 145

A **PAIR WORK** Use the language in the grammar box to talk about these signs.

A: This first sign means you've got to use the stairs in case of a fire.
B: Yes, I think you're right. And the second one means you aren't allowed to . . .

B **CLASS ACTIVITY** What are some of the rules in your office or school?

A: In my office, we can't eat at our desks.
B: We can't either, but we're allowed to have water.
C: We're allowed to eat at our desks, but we have to clean up afterward.

10 DISCUSSION Play by the rules.

A PAIR WORK How many rules can you think of for each of these places?

at the gym	at a public swimming pool	on an airplane
in a museum	in a movie theater	at work

"At the gym, you have to wear sneakers or other athletic shoes. You're not allowed to wear regular shoes."

B GROUP WORK Share your ideas. Why do you think these rules exist? Have you ever broken any of them? What happened?

11 LISTENING Road signs

A Listen to four conversations about driving. Number the situations they are discussing in the correct order from 1 to 4.

___ Cars can't be in the bus and taxi lane.
___ Drivers must drive within the speed limit.
___ Drivers have to turn on car headlights on mountain roads.
___ Cars are allowed to park in this area after 6:00 P.M.

B Listen again. How did they find out about the traffic situation? Write what happened.

1. _____
2. _____
3. _____
4. _____

C PAIR WORK How do you move around your city? Give two examples of traffic laws you must obey.

12 WRITING Golden rules

A GROUP WORK Discuss the rules that currently exist at your school. How many can you think of? Are they all good rules?

B GROUP WORK Think of four new rules that you feel would be a good idea. Work together to write brief explanations of why each is necessary.

> 1. You aren't allowed to use your first language. If you need to use it, you need to ask your teacher for permission.
> 2. You have to pay a small fine if you hand in your homework late.
> 3. You can be late, but you have to come in quietly so you don't disturb the lesson.

C CLASS ACTIVITY Share your lists. Vote on the best new rules.

13 READING

A Skim the article. Match the pictures 1, 2, and 3 to the paragraphs.

UNDERSTANDING IDIOMS

Idioms can be a problem for language learners. They often seem to make absolutely no sense at all. For example, imagine your English friend Sam tells you his math exam was "a piece of cake." Do you imagine him at school, sitting in front of a sweet dessert with nothing but a pen to eat it with? In fact, he's saying that the exam was really easy. It's important to learn useful English idioms and knowing their origins helps us to remember them. Here are stories of three English idioms.

___ **A** If you ask a friend to hang out, you might hear, "Sorry, I can't tonight. I'm feeling a little under the weather." It may sound like rain is coming, but really, it means that your friend feels sick. This expression came from sailors, who often got seasick when bad weather tossed the ship from side to side. The sailors went down to the bottom part of the ship, away from the storm and where the ship's rocking was gentler.

___ **B** If you have a difficult roommate, you might say, "My roommate has loud parties every night, but last night was the last straw. They played music till 5 A.M.! I'm moving out." A "last straw" is a final problem that makes someone take action. This expression is a short form of the phrase "the straw that broke the camel's back." The idea is that even though a single piece of straw is very light, many pieces added together will be too heavy for the camel to carry.

___ **C** Have you ever asked someone if they know something, and they reply, "That rings a bell"? They're not hearing music! They mean that what you're saying sounds familiar, and they think they've heard it before. This idiom comes from the fact that bells are used to remind people of many things. Traditionally, bells would toll for an important event, like a wedding. School bells tell you that class is starting, and even the alarm chime on your phone reminds you that it's time to get up.

B Read the article and correct the false statements below.

1. You can guess the meaning of an idiom if you understand each word.
   _____
2. In the past, people knew about important events when they heard shouting.
   _____
3. A camel falls down if it has to carry too much water.
   _____
4. Sailors used to feel sicker when they went to the bottom of the ship.
   _____

C Complete the sentences with the correct form of one of the idioms.

1. Julie has a bad cold at the moment, and she's _____.
2. I don't remember his face, but his name _____.
3. When the neighbors' noisy kids broke my window with their ball, it _____.

D What idioms are commonly used in your country? Where do you think they come from?

Now I get it!

Units 13–14 Progress check

SELF-ASSESSMENT

How well can you do these things? Check (✓) the boxes.

I can . . .	Very well	OK	A little
Ask about and express opinions and emotions (Ex. 1, 4, 5)	☐	☐	☐
Discuss movies (Ex. 2)	☐	☐	☐
Understand descriptions of rules and laws (Ex. 3)	☐	☐	☐
Speculate about things when I'm not sure and recognize emotions (Ex. 4)	☐	☐	☐
Describe rules and laws: permission, obligation, and prohibition (Ex. 5)	☐	☐	☐

1 SURVEY Personal preferences

A Complete the first column of the survey with your opinions.

	Me	My classmate
A fascinating book		
A confusing movie		
A boring TV show		
A shocking news story		
An interesting celebrity		
A singer you are amazed by		
A song you are annoyed by		

B **CLASS ACTIVITY** Go around the class and find someone who has the same opinions. Write a classmate's name only once.

"I thought *I am Malala* was a fascinating book. What about you?"

2 ROLE PLAY Movie night

Student A: Invite Student B to a movie. Suggest two movie options.
Then answer your partner's questions.
Start like this: *Do you want to see a movie?*

Student B: Student A invites you to a movie.
Find out more about the movie.
Then accept or refuse the invitation.

Change roles and try the role play again.

3 LISTENING Unusual laws around the world

A Listen to two people discuss an article about laws in different places. Match the topic to the place. (There are two extra topics.)

a. smiling	b. chewing gum	c. stealing
d. hospitals	e. pigeons	f. carrying money

1. Singapore ____
2. Kenya ____
3. San Francisco ____
4. Milan ____

B Listen again. Complete the sentences to describe each law.

1. In Singapore, you _____.
2. In Kenya, you _____.
3. In San Francisco, you _____.
4. In Milan, you _____.

C PAIR WORK Which law seems the strangest to you? the most logical? Why?

4 GAME Miming

A Think of two emotions or ideas you can communicate with gestures. Write them on separate cards.

B GROUP WORK Shuffle your cards together. Then take turns picking cards and acting out the meanings with gestures. The student who guesses correctly goes next.

A: That probably means you're disgusted.
B: No.
C: It could mean you're surprised.
B: You're getting closer . . .

I'm confused. I don't understand what you really want.

5 DISCUSSION What's the law?

GROUP WORK Read these laws from the United States. What do you think about them? Are they the same or different in your country?

- You aren't allowed to keep certain wild animals as pets.
- You're allowed to vote when you turn 18.
- In some states, you can get married when you're 16.
- You have to wear a seat belt in the back seat of a car in most states.
- Young men don't have to serve in the military.
- In some states, you can't drive faster than 65 miles per hour (about 100 kph).
- In most states, children have to attend school until they are 16 or 18.

A: In the U.S.A., you aren't allowed to keep certain wild animals as pets.
B: It's the same for us. You've got to have a special permit to keep a wild animal.
C: I've heard that in some countries, you can keep lions and tigers as pets.

WHAT'S NEXT?

Look at your Self-assessment again. Do you need to review anything?

15 I wouldn't have done that.

▶ Discuss imaginary situations
▶ Discuss difficult situations

1 SNAPSHOT

NEWS 4 YOU   NEW TODAY   MOST POPULAR   TRENDING   LOGIN | SIGN UP

FLORIDA MOM "CAUGHT" BEING HONEST
Nancy Bloom was caught on the security camera entering a convenience store while the owner was out to lunch. The door was unlocked, so Nancy walked in with her son, picked up some ice cream, and left the money on the counter.

MOST SHARED THIS WEEK

HONESTY IS ITS OWN REWARD
After driving for 20 miles to return a wallet lost in a park, Kate Moore gets only a half-hearted, "Oh. Thanks."

HOMELESS MAN FINDS $40,000 AND TURNS IT IN
When Tom Heart found a backpack full of cash, he didn't think twice. He took it straight to the police. After reading Tom's story, a stranger started a fundraising campaign for Tom that has already raised over $60,000.

Have you heard any stories like these recently?
Have you ever found anything valuable? What did you do?
Do you think that people who return lost things should get a reward?

2 CONVERSATION What would you do?

A Listen and practice.

Joon: Look at this. A homeless guy found a backpack with $40,000 inside!
Mia: And what did he do?
Joon: He took it to the police. He gave it all back, every single penny.
Mia: You're kidding! If I found $40,000, I wouldn't return it. I'd keep it.
Joon: Really? What would you do with it?
Mia: Well, I'd spend it. I could buy a new car or take a nice long vacation.
Joon: The real owner might find out about it, though, and then you could go to jail.
Mia: Hmm. You've got a point there.

B Listen to the rest of the conversation. What would Joon do if he found $40,000?

3 GRAMMAR FOCUS

Unreal conditional sentences with *if* clauses

Imaginary situation (simple past)	Possible consequence (*would*, *could*, or *might* + verb)
If I **found** $40,000,	I **would keep** it. I **wouldn't return** it. I **could buy** a new car. I **might go** to the police.

What **would** you **do if** you **found** $40,000?

GRAMMAR PLUS see page 146

A Complete these conversations. Then compare with a partner.

1. **A:** What _____ you _____ (do) if you lost your sister's favorite sweater?
   B: Of course I _____ (buy) her a new one.
2. **A:** If you _____ (have) three months to travel, where _____ you _____ (go)?
   B: Oh, that's easy! I _____ (fly) to Europe. I've always wanted to go there.
3. **A:** If your doctor _____ (tell) you to get more exercise, which activity _____ you _____ (choose)?
   B: I'm not sure, but I think I _____ (go) jogging two or three times a week.
4. **A:** _____ you _____ (break) into your house if you _____ (lock) yourself out?
   B: No way! If I _____ (not have) another key, I _____ (ask) a neighbor for help.
5. **A:** If your friend _____ (want) to marry someone you didn't like, _____ you _____ (say) something?
   B: No, I _____ (not say) anything. I _____ (mind) my own business.
6. **A:** What _____ you _____ (do) if you _____ (see) your favorite movie star on the street?
   B: I _____ (not be) shy! I _____ (ask) to take a photo with them.

B **PAIR WORK** Take turns asking the questions in part A. Answer with your own information.

4 LISTENING Tough situations

A Listen to three people talk about predicaments. Check which predicament they are talking about.

1. ☐ Chris has relationship problems.   ☐ Chris is addicted to the Internet.
2. ☐ Kari spent all her money in Europe.   ☐ Kari lost all her money in Europe.
3. ☐ Zoey saw her classmates cheating.   ☐ Zoey doesn't understand her math class.

B Listen again. Write the two suggestions given for each predicament.

1. a. _____   b. _____
2. a. _____   b. _____
3. a. _____   b. _____

C **GROUP WORK** Which suggestions do you agree with? Why?

5 INTERCHANGE 15 Tough choices

What would you do in some difficult situations? Go to Interchange 15 on page 130.

6 WORD POWER Opposites

A Find nine pairs of opposites in this list. Complete the chart. Then compare with a partner.

accept	borrow	dislike	find	lose	remember
admit	deny	divorce	forget	marry	save
agree	disagree	enjoy	lend	refuse	spend

accept	≠	refuse		≠			≠	
	≠			≠			≠	
	≠			≠			≠	

B **PAIR WORK** Choose four pairs of opposites. Write sentences using each pair.

> I can't remember my dreams. As soon as I wake up, I forget them.

7 PERSPECTIVES That was a big mistake.

A Listen to people talk about recent predicaments. Then check (✓) the best suggestion for each one.

> "I borrowed my sister's brand new car, and I scratched it while I was parking. I didn't want her to be upset with me, so I told her the scratch was there already. What should I have done?"

☐ You should have told her about it.
☐ You should have taken it to a repair shop.
☐ You should have offered to pay for the damage.

> "I forgot my best friend's birthday. I felt terrible, so I texted him to apologize, but he's still upset. What would you have done?"

☐ I would have called him right away.
☐ I would have sent him a nice birthday present.
☐ I would have invited him out for a meal.

B **PAIR WORK** Compare with a partner. Do you agree with each other?

Unit 15

8 GRAMMAR FOCUS

Past modals

Use *would have* or *should have* + past participle to give opinions or suggestions about actions in the past.

What **should** I **have done**?   You **should have told** her about it.
                                  You **shouldn't have lied** to your sister.

What **would** you **have done**? I **would have called** him.
                                   I **wouldn't have texted** him.

GRAMMAR PLUS see page 146

A Complete these conversations. Then practice with a partner.

1. **A:** I was in a meeting at work when my girlfriend texted me saying she needed to see me right away. What should I have _____ (do)?
   B: You should have _____ (send) her a message and _____ (tell) her you'd call back later.

2. **A:** The cashier gave me too much change. What should I have _____ (do)?
   B: You should have _____ (say) something. You shouldn't have _____ (take) the money.

3. **A:** I ignored an email from someone I don't like. What would you have _____ (do)?
   B: I would have _____ (reply) to the person. It just takes a minute!

4. **A:** We left all our trash at the campsite. What would you have _____ (do)?
   B: I would have _____ (take) it with me and _____ (throw) it away later.

B Read the situations below. What would have been the best thing to do? Choose suggestions. Then compare with a partner.

Situations

1. The teacher borrowed my favorite book and spilled coffee all over it. _____
2. I saw a classmate cheating on an exam, so I wrote her an email about it. _____
3. A friend of mine always has messy hair, so I gave him a comb for his birthday. _____
4. I hit someone's car when I was leaving a parking lot. Luckily, no one saw me. _____
5. My aunt gave me a wool sweater. I can't wear wool, so I gave it back. _____

Suggestions

a. You should have spoken to him about it.
b. I would have spoken to the teacher about it.
c. I would have waited for the owner to return.
d. I wouldn't have said anything.
e. You should have warned her not to do it again.
f. You should have left a note for the owner.
g. I would have told her that I prefer something else.
h. You should have exchanged it for something else.

C GROUP WORK Make another suggestion for each situation in part B.

9 PRONUNCIATION Reduction of *have*

A Listen and practice. Notice how *have* is reduced in these sentences.

/əv/
What would you have done?

/əv/
I would have told the truth.

B PAIR WORK Practice the conversations in Exercise 8, part A, again. Use the reduced form of *have*.

I wouldn't have done that.

10 LISTENING Problem solved!

A Listen to an advice podcast. Complete the chart.

	Problem	What the person did
Ronnie:		
Becca:		

B Listen again. According to Dr. Jones, what should each person have done?

Ronnie: _____

Becca: _____

C PAIR WORK What would you have done in each situation?

11 SPEAKING An awful trip

A PAIR WORK Imagine a friend has been on a really awful trip and everything went wrong. What should your friend have done? What shouldn't he or she have done?

Your friend spent hours in the sun and got a sunburn.
Your friend drank tap water and got sick.
Your friend stayed at a very bad hotel.
Your friend's wallet was stolen.
Your friend overslept and missed the flight back.

A: She shouldn't have spent so many hours in the sun.
B: She should have used sunscreen.

B GROUP WORK Have you ever had any bad experiences on a trip? What happened?

12 WRITING Advice needed

Write a post to a community blog about a real or imaginary problem.
Put your drafts on the wall and choose one to write a reply to.

WHAT WENT WRONG?
submitted by dmartin 10 hours ago

I lent my girlfriend $10,000 to help her pay for her college tuition. That was about a year ago, and at the time, she said she would pay me back as soon as she found a job. She never even looked for a job. Last week, I asked her for my money back, and she accused me of being selfish, unsympathetic, and insensitive. She broke up with me, and now she won't even talk to me anymore. What did I do wrong? What should I have done? What should I do now? Does anyone have any suggestions?

248 comments

13 READING

A Skim the three posts. What do Jack, Maya, and Andrés ask for advice about?

TOPTIPS.COM

HOME   NEW   ABOUT   COMMUNITY   SIGN IN

1 JACK – LONDON ♡12

I am overweight, and I'd really like to slim down. I've tried all kinds of diets, but none of them seem to work. And there's so much advice on the Internet – I don't know what to believe any more. What would you recommend?

I had the same problem until I tried a high protein/no carbohydrate diet. It was very strict – in the first couple of weeks you have to eat less than 40 grams of carbohydrates a day, so no bread, pasta, or potatoes! But I lost nine pounds in just 13 days, so for me it was worth it. I had a lot of meat and eggs and some butter, too, which was great! I'd give it a shot if I were you. (Sarah, Edinburgh)

2 MAYA – SAN FRANCISCO ♡22

I'm traveling to Rio de Janeiro next month, and I'd like to see as much of the city as possible. The problem is that I'm only going to be there for a couple of days, and I'm not sure how to fit everything in. Should I book an organized tour?

I was in Rio a couple of months ago. I travel a lot and like to be independent, so I chose to find my own way around the city. What a mistake! Rio's so big that I kept getting lost! And in the end, I didn't get to see the beach of Ipanema or the cathedral. It would have been nice to have somebody to talk to also. I really should have gone on a guided tour. (Dag, Oslo)

3 ANDRÉS – BOGOTÁ ♡11

I've just finished my degree, and I'm on the fence about what to do next. Here in Bogotá, there aren't many job possibilities right now. Should I go back to college to get a Master's? Or go stay with my cousin in New York and try to get a job there? (My English is not very good, by the way – a friend wrote this!)

Stay where you are! I moved to the United States from Poland and got a job as a server, but it's long hours and not much money. I haven't really made many friends, and I miss home. I should have stayed there and continued with my studies. (Marta, Krakow)

B Read the posts. Who would say these sentences? Write names from the posts.

1. Should I go abroad or stay where I am? _____
2. It worked for me, so why don't you try it? _____
3. I would have been happier if I hadn't moved. _____
4. How can I choose the right eating plan? _____
5. If I went there again, I'd definitely join a group. _____
6. I don't have much time, so I need to be organized. _____

C Find words or expressions in the posts to match these definitions.

1. Be an important or useful thing to do (post 1) _____
2. Find enough time for something (post 2) _____
3. To be unable to make a decision (post 3) _____

D Do you agree with the advice given above? What advice would you give?

I wouldn't have done that. **105**

16 Making excuses

▶ Give reasons and explanations
▶ Discuss statements other people made

1 SNAPSHOT

Good Excuses, Poor Excuses

Not doing homework
- I was sure the assignment was due tomorrow.
- I emailed it to you, but it bounced back.

Arriving late to class
- My father didn't wake me up.
- My bike tire was flat because a dog bit it.

Missing work
- My cat was sick, and I had to take care of her.
- It was my birthday, and I always donate blood on that day.

Arriving late to work
- I worked on the new project until four in the morning, and then I overslept.
- My wife thinks it's funny to hide my car keys in the morning.

Arriving late for a date
- I was taking a telephone survey and lost track of the time.
- A horse running on the highway was holding up traffic.

Which are good excuses? Which are poor ones?
What excuse do you usually use for these situations?
What excuses can you make for missing a date or party?

2 PERSPECTIVES At your request

A Who do you think made these requests? Listen and match.

1. She said to arrive on time for the meeting. ___
2. She asked me to pick up some food on the way home. ___
3. He said not to miss practice again. ___
4. She told me to hand in my homework before Friday. ___
5. She said to drink at least six glasses of water a day. ___
6. He asked me not to tell Mom about his new girlfriend. ___
7. He told me not to leave my bike in the apartment hallway. ___

a. my teacher
b. my boss
c. my brother
d. my doctor
e. my neighbor
f. my roommate
g. my coach

B **PAIR WORK** Can you think of another request each person might make?

A: Our teacher sometimes says, "Open your books."
B: A teacher could also say, "Repeat after me."

106

3 GRAMMAR FOCUS

> **Reported speech: requests**

Original request	Reported request
Arrive on time for the meeting.	She **said to arrive** on time for the meeting.
	She **told me to arrive** on time for the meeting.
Don't leave your bike in the apartment hallway.	He **said not to leave** my bike in the hallway.
	He **told me not to leave** my bike in the hallway.
Can you pick up some food on the way home?	She **asked me to pick up** some food.

GRAMMAR PLUS see page 147

A Victor is organizing a surprise birthday party for his teacher. Look at what he told his classmates. Write each request using *say*, *tell*, or *ask*. Then compare with a partner.

1. Meet at my apartment at 7:30.   *He told them to meet at his apartment at 7:30.*
2. Don't arrive late.
3. Can you bring some ice cream?
4. Can you help me make the sandwiches?
5. Can you bring a small gift for her?
6. Don't spend more than $10 on the gift.
7. Keep the party a secret.
8. Don't say anything to the other teachers.

B GROUP WORK Imagine you're planning a class party. Write four requests. Then take turns reading your requests and changing them into reported requests.

Edu: Bring something to eat to the party!
Eva: Edu told us to bring something to eat.

Aki: Can you help me clean up after the party?
Jim: Aki asked us to help her clean up.

4 SPEAKING That's asking too much!

A Think of requests that people have made recently. Write two things people asked you to do and two things people asked you *not* to do.

Person	Request
My boss	shave off my beard

B GROUP WORK Talk about the requests that each of you listed in part A. Did you do what people requested? Did you give an excuse? What was it?

Making excuses

5 WORD POWER Verb-noun collocations

A Find three more nouns that are usually paired with each verb. The same noun can be paired with more than one verb. Then compare with a partner.

an apology	an invitation	a request
a complaint	a joke	a solution
an excuse	a lie	a story
an explanation	an offer	a suggestion
an idea	a reason	the truth

make	_a request_	_____	_____	_____	_____
give	_an excuse_	_____	_____	_____	_____
tell	_a joke_	_____	_____	_____	_____
accept	_an apology_	_____	_____	_____	_____
refuse	_an invitation_	_____	_____	_____	_____

B **PAIR WORK** How do you deal with the things in part A? Tell a partner.

A: What do you do when a close friend makes a difficult request?
B: I give a good explanation, and I offer to help in another way. What about you?

6 CONVERSATION Are you doing anything on Sunday?

A Listen and practice.

Gabriel: Hi, Craig.

Craig: Oh, hi, Gabriel. How are things?

Gabriel: Just fine, thanks. Uh, are you doing anything on Sunday night?

Craig: Hmm. Sunday night? Let me think. Oh, yes. My brother just called, and he told me he had tickets to the basketball finals. I said I would go with him.

Gabriel: Oh, that's too bad! It's my birthday. I'm having dinner with Tina, and I thought I'd invite more people and make it a party.

Craig: Oh, I'm really sorry, but I won't be able to make it.

Gabriel: I'm sorry, too. But that's OK.

B **PAIR WORK** Act out the conversation in part A. Make up your own excuse for not accepting Gabriel's invitation.

7 LISTENING Making excuses

A Listen to Gabriel invite his friends to his birthday party on Saturday. What excuses do they give for not going? Write them below.

1. Grant: _____
2. Sayo: _____
3. Diego: _____
4. Carrie: _____

B Listen. What happens on the night of Gabriel's birthday?

C PAIR WORK What was the last party you went to? Describe it to your partner.

8 GRAMMAR FOCUS

Reported speech: statements

Direct statements	Reported statements
I'm not feeling well.	She said (that) she wasn't feeling well.
I have houseguests for the weekend.	she had houseguests for the weekend.
I made a tennis date with Kim.	she had made a tennis date with Kim.
I have planned an exciting trip.	she had planned an exciting trip.
We can't come tomorrow.	They told me (that) they couldn't come tomorrow.
We will be out of town.	they would be out of town.
We may go out with friends.	they might go out with friends.

GRAMMAR PLUS see page 147

A Isabella is having a party at her house on Saturday. Look at these excuses. Change them into reported speech. Then compare with a partner.

1. Mason: "I already have plans for Saturday."
2. Olivia: "My in-laws are coming over for dinner that night."
3. Ben and Ava: "We've been invited to a graduation party on Saturday."
4. Felipe: "I promised to help my sister with her homework."
5. Tae-yun: "I can't come because I broke my leg."
6. Osvaldo: "I'll be moving this weekend."
7. Lisa and Henry: "We have to pick someone up at the airport that evening."
8. Omar: "I may have to work the night shift on Saturday."

Mason said he already had plans for Saturday. OR
Mason told her he already had plans for Saturday.

B GROUP WORK Imagine you don't want to go to Isabella's party. Take turns making excuses and changing them into reported speech.

A: I'm sorry, I can't go. I'm going camping this weekend.
B: Lucky guy! He said he was going camping this weekend.

9 PRONUNCIATION Reduction of *had* and *would*

A Listen and practice. Notice how *had* and *would* are reduced in the following sentences.

She said she**'d made** the bed. (She said she **had made** the bed.)
She said she**'d make** the bed. (She said she **would make** the bed.)

B Listen to four sentences. Check (✓) the reduced form that you hear.

1. ☐ had 2. ☐ had 3. ☐ had 4. ☐ had
   ☐ would ☐ would ☐ would ☐ would

10 WRITING About my classmates

A Interview your classmates and take notes. Use your notes to write a report describing what people told you. Use reported speech.

	Name	Response
What did you do last night?		
What movie have you seen recently?		
Where are you going after class?		
What are your plans for the weekend?		
What will you do on your next birthday?		

B GROUP WORK Read your report, but don't give names. Others guess the person.

"Someone said that he'd go to Paris on his next vacation."

11 SPEAKING You can make it.

A GROUP WORK What are some things you would like to do in the future? Think of three intentions.

A: I'm going to take an English course abroad.
B: That sounds fun. Have you decided where?

B CLASS ACTIVITY Report the best intentions you heard. Then give suggestions.

B: Noriko said she was going to take an English course abroad, but she hadn't decided where.
C: She could go to Australia. My brother attended a very good school there. He told me he studied incredibly hard!

12 INTERCHANGE 16 Just a bunch of excuses

Make some plans. Student A, go to Interchange 16A on page 129;
Student B, go to Interchange 16B on page 131.

13 READING

A Scan the article. What are three common reasons for missing work?

A GOOD EXCUSE FOR A DAY OFF WORK

1 On average, U.S. employees take 4.9 sick days per year. Usually this does not cause any particular problems. But when employees take sick leave without a good reason, it can quickly become an issue. In fact, in one survey, 18 percent of employers said that they had fired an employee for taking days off without a good reason. The key is to understand what reasons are acceptable and what reasons are not. Generally, most excuses for sick days fall into one of three categories.

2 The most common reasons for not going to work are health-related. It would probably be OK to tell your boss that you ate something bad last night and that you have a stomachache. Of course you might not want to share the details of a health issue with your boss – after all, you do have the right to privacy. If you don't want to be too specific, you can just tell your boss that you have a small medical issue and need to take the day off.

3 Household accidents are the second category of reasons for not going in to work. You might call your boss to say you slipped in the shower and hurt your knee. This is a common accident and one that your boss will sympathize with. However, if you are going to be out of work for several days due to an injury, it's important to make arrangements with your employer. See if you can work from home, or at least make sure there is someone to cover your work.

4 The third type of sick day use isn't really about illness, but it's about something else you can't control: transportation problems. The car might not start, there may be a terrible traffic jam, or there could be delays on the subway. Some employers may be sympathetic to absences due to transportation problems, but others may not. It's important to know your boss and to understand whether he or she will accept an excuse like this.

5 Regardless of the reason for the sick day, there are a few things you can do to make missing work more acceptable to your employer. Try to keep sick days to a minimum. When you do need to take a sick day, give your employer as much advance notice as possible. Finally, never take a sick day if there isn't anything wrong with you – the only good excuses are the ones that are true.

B Read the article. Then correct four mistakes in the summary of the article.

U.S. workers take just under a month in sick days a year. The least frequently used excuses are for health reasons. When employees take a sick day, it's important to explain the reason to their colleagues. It's OK to take a sick day, even if you feel fine, as long as you give an excuse.

C Find words in the text to match these definitions.

1. told someone to leave his or her job (paragraph 1) _____
2. an explanation given for something (paragraph 1) _____
3. someone's right to keep information about his or her personal life secret (paragraph 2) _____
4. understand or care about someone's problems (paragraph 3) _____
5. a warning that something is about to happen (paragraph 5) _____

D What other excuses do people make for not going to work or class? What's the silliest excuse you have ever heard?

Making excuses

Units 15–16 Progress check

SELF-ASSESSMENT

How well can you do these things? Check (✓) the boxes.

I can . . .	Very well	OK	A little
Discuss imaginary events (Ex. 1)	☐	☐	☐
Ask for and give advice and suggestions about past events (Ex. 2)	☐	☐	☐
Understand and report requests (Ex. 3)	☐	☐	☐
Discuss statements other people made (Ex. 4)	☐	☐	☐

1 DISCUSSION Interesting situations

A What would you do in these situations? Complete the statements.

If I forgot to do my homework, _____.
If I found a valuable piece of jewelry in the park, _____.
If a friend gave me a present I didn't like, _____.
If I wasn't invited to a party I wanted to attend, _____.
If someone took my clothes while I was swimming, _____.

B GROUP WORK Compare your responses. For each situation, choose one to tell the class.

A: What would you do if you forgot to do your homework?
B: I'd probably tell the teacher the truth. I'd ask her to let me hand it in next class.

2 SPEAKING Predicaments

A Make up two situations like the one below. Think about experiences you have had or heard about at work, home, or school.

"An old friend from high school visited me recently. We had a great time at first, but he became annoying. He made a big mess, and he left his things all over the place. After two weeks, I told him he had to leave because my sister was coming for the weekend."

B PAIR WORK Take turns sharing your situations. Ask for advice and suggestions.

A: What would you have done?
B: Well, I would have told him to pick up his clothes, and I would have asked him to clean up his mess.

3 LISTENING A small request

A Listen to the conversations. Check (✓) the person who is making the request.

1. ☐ child   2. ☐ neighbor   3. ☐ child   4. ☐ teacher   5. ☐ boss   6. ☐ neighbor
   ☐ parent   ☐ teacher   ☐ doctor   ☐ classmate   ☐ neighbor   ☐ teacher

B Listen again. Complete the requests.

1. Please _____ .
2. Can _____ ?
3. Don't _____ .
4. Can _____ ?
5. Please _____ .
6. Can _____ ?

C **PAIR WORK** Work with a partner. Imagine these requests were for you. Take turns reporting the requests to your partner.

"My dad told me to pick up my things."

4 GAME Who is lying?

A Think of situations when you expressed anger, gave an excuse, or made a complaint. Write a brief statement about each situation.

I once complained about the bathroom in a hotel.

B **CLASS ACTIVITY** Play a game. Choose three students to be contestants.

Step 1: The contestants compare their statements and choose one. This statement should be true about only one student. The other two students should pretend they had the experience.

Step 2: The contestants stand in front of the class. Each contestant reads the same statement. The rest of the class must ask questions to find out who isn't telling the truth.

Contestant A, what hotel were you in?

Contestant B, what was wrong with the bathroom?

Contestant C, what did the manager do?

Step 3: Who isn't telling the truth? What did he or she say to make you think that?
"I don't think Contestant B is telling the truth. He said the bathroom was too small!"

WHAT'S NEXT?

Look at your Self-assessment again. Do you need to review anything?

Interchange activities

INTERCHANGE 1 We have a lot in common.

A CLASS ACTIVITY Go around the class and find out the information below. Then ask follow-up questions and take notes. Write a classmate's name only once.

Find someone who . . .	Name	Notes
1. wanted to be a movie star **"Did you ever want to be a movie star?"**		
2. always listened to his or her teachers **"Did you always listen to your teachers?"**		
3. used to look very different **"Did you use to look very different?"**		
4. had a pet when he or she was little **"Did you have a pet when you were little?"**		
5. changed schools when he or she was a child "_____?"		
6. used to argue with his or her brothers and sisters "_____?"		
7. got in trouble a lot as a child "_____?"		
8. used to have a favorite toy "_____?"		

B GROUP WORK Tell the group the most interesting thing you learned about your classmates.

INTERCHANGE 2 Top travel destinations

A PAIR WORK Look at the photos and slogans below. What do you think the theme of each tourism campaign is?

Possible themes

art	culture	entertainment
food	history	music
nature	shopping	sports

Cartagena
"The Colorful Caribbean"

New Orleans
"The Birthplace of Jazz"

Cairo
"The Earth's Mother"

Bangkok
"Thailand Old and New"

B GROUP WORK Imagine you are planning a campaign to attract more tourists to one of the cities above or to a city of your choice. Use the ideas below or your own ideas to discuss the campaign.

a good time to visit
famous historical attractions
special events or festivals
nice areas to stay
interesting places to see
memorable things to do

A: Do you know when a good time to visit Cartagena is?
B: I think between December and April is a good time because . . .

C GROUP WORK What will be the theme of your campaign? What slogan will you use?

Interchange 2

INTERCHANGE 3 A dream come true

A Complete this questionnaire with information about yourself.

My Wish List

1. What possession do you wish you had?
   I wish I had _____

2. What sport do you wish you could play?
   _____

3. Where do you wish you could live?
   _____

4. What skill do you wish you had?
   _____

5. What kind of home do you wish you could have?
   _____

6. What kind of vacation do you wish you could take?
   _____

7. What languages do you wish you could speak?
   _____

8. Which musical instruments do you wish you could play?
   _____

9. What famous person do you wish you could meet?
   _____

10. What kind of pet do you wish you could have?
    _____

B **PAIR WORK** Compare your questionnaires. Take turns asking and answering questions about your wishes.

A: What possession do you wish you had?
B: I wish I had a sailboat.
A: Really? Why?
B: Well, I could sail around the world!

C **CLASS ACTIVITY** Imagine you are at a class reunion. It is ten years since you completed the questionnaire in part A. Tell the class about some wishes that have come true for your partner.

"Victor is now a famous explorer and sailor. He has sailed across the Atlantic and to the South Pole. Right now, he's writing a book about his adventures on his boat."

INTERCHANGE 4 Oh, really?

A How much do you really know about your classmates? Look at the survey and add two more situations to items 1 and 2.

	Name	Notes
1. Find someone who has . . . a. cooked for more than twenty people b. found something valuable c. lost his or her phone d. been on TV e. cried during a movie f. _____ g. _____		
2. Find someone who has never . . . a. been camping b. gone horseback riding c. fallen asleep at the movies d. played a video game e. baked cookies f. _____ g. _____		

B **CLASS ACTIVITY** Go around the class and ask the questions. Write the names of classmates who answer "yes" for item 1 and "no" for item 2. Then ask follow-up questions and take notes.

A: Have you ever cooked for more than 20 people?
B: Yes, I have. Last year I cooked for the whole family on Mother's Day.
A: How was it?
B: Well, my mother had to help me.

A: Have you ever been camping?
C: No, I haven't.
A: Why not?
C: Because I don't like mosquitoes.

C **GROUP WORK** Compare the information in your surveys.

Interchange 4

INTERCHANGE 5A Fun trips

STUDENT A

A PAIR WORK You and your partner are going to take a trip. You have a brochure for a surfing trip to Hawaii, and your partner has a brochure for a hiking trip to the Grand Canyon.

First, find out about the hiking trip. Ask your partner questions about these things.

The length of the trip	The cost of the trip	What the price includes
The accommodations	Additional activities	Nighttime activities

B PAIR WORK Now use the information in this brochure to answer your partner's questions about the surfing trip.

SURFING VACATION IN HAWAII

Seven-day surf camp on the magical island of Oahu for surfers of all ability levels

Visit the best attractions on the island:
Kailua Beach Park
The Waikiki Aquarium
Pearl Harbor

Accommodations:
Beachfront studios and apartments

Price includes:
Daily surf lessons
All necessary equipment
Breakfast and lunch

Additional activities:
Catamaran sailing lessons
Snorkeling at Hanauma Bay Beach

Nighttime activities:
Authentic Hawaiian luau
Hula shows

Vacation cost:
$2,100

C PAIR WORK Decide which trip you are going to take. Then explain your choice to the class.

INTERCHANGE 6 I'm terribly sorry.

A **PAIR WORK** Look at these situations. Act out conversations. Apologize and then give an excuse, admit a mistake, or make an offer or a promise.

useful expressions	
I'm sorry. / I didn't realize. / I forgot.	You're right. / I was wrong.
I'll . . . right away.	I'll make sure to . . . / I promise I'll . . .

1

Student A: You are trying to watch the movie.
Student B: You are talking on your phone.
A: Excuse me. I'm trying to watch the movie. Could you please turn off your phone?
B: I'm so sorry . . .

2

Student A: You are the server.
Student B: You are one of the customers.
A: Oh, I'm terribly sorry . . .
B: _____

3

Student A: You have just arrived for the meeting.
Student B: You are making a presentation.
A: I'm sorry I'm late . . .
B: _____

4

Student A: You are the host.
Student B: You broke the vase.
A: Oh, no! My vase.
B: _____

B **GROUP WORK** Have you ever experienced situations like these? What happened? What did you do? Share your stories.

Interchange 6

INTERCHANGE 5B Fun trips

Student B

A PAIR WORK You and your partner are going to take a trip. You have a brochure for a hiking trip to the Grand Canyon, and your partner has a brochure for a surfing trip to Hawaii.

First, use the information in the brochure to answer your partner's questions about the hiking trip.

HIKING TRIP IN THE GRAND CANYON

Ten-day tour of spectacular sights with knowledgeable, friendly tour guides

Places to visit:
The red rock canyons
Zion National Park
The Navajo Nation
Kaibab National Forest

Accommodations:
Single or double rooms at historic lodges inside the national park

Price includes:
Breakfast and dinner every day
Two picnic lunches
Transportation to all attractions

Additional activities:
Rafting the Colorado River
Helicopter tour
Lake Powell boat cruise

Nighttime activities:
Dinner cruise
Stargazing
Campfire sing-alongs

Vacation cost:
$1,980

B PAIR WORK Now find out about the surfing trip. Ask your partner questions about these things.

The length of the trip	The cost of the trip	What the price includes
The accommodations	Additional activities	Nighttime activities

C PAIR WORK Decide which trip you are going to take. Then explain your choice to the class.

INTERCHANGE 7 Free advice

A GROUP WORK Look at the problems people have. What advice would you give each person? Discuss possible suggestions and then choose the best one.

1. "I'm moving to a new apartment with two roommates. How can I be sure we get along well and avoid problems?"

2. "A co-worker has asked to borrow my brand-new mountain bike for the weekend. I don't want to lend it. What can I say?"

3. "My family and I are going away on vacation for two weeks. How can we make sure our home is safe from burglars while we're gone?"

4. "I have an important job interview next week. How can I make sure to be successful and get the job?"

5. "I'm going to meet my future in-laws tomorrow for the first time. How can I make a good impression?"

6. "I'm really into social networking, but in the past week, five people I hardly know have asked to be my friends. What should I do?"

B PAIR WORK Choose one of the situations above. Ask your partner for advice. Then give him or her advice about his or her problem.

A: I'm moving to a new apartment with two roommates. How can I be sure we get along well?
B: Make sure you decide how you are going to split the household chores. And remember to . . .

Interchange 7 121

INTERCHANGE 8 It's worth celebrating.

A CLASS ACTIVITY How do your classmates celebrate special occasions? Go around the class and ask the questions below. If someone answers "yes," write down his or her name. Ask for more information and take notes.

Question	Name	Notes
1. Have you ever given someone a surprise party?		
2. What's the best gift you have ever received?		
3. Do you ever wear traditional clothes?		
4. Have you bought flowers for someone special recently?		
5. Do you like to watch parades?		
6. Does your family have big get-togethers?		
7. Has someone given you money recently as a gift?		
8. Will you celebrate your next birthday with a party?		
9. Do you ever give friends birthday presents?		
10. What's your favorite time of the year?		
11. Do you ever celebrate a holiday with fireworks?		

A: Have you ever given someone a surprise party?
B: Yes. Once we gave my co-worker a surprise party on his birthday.
A: How was it?
B: It was great. He never suspected that we were planning it, so he was really surprised. And he was very happy that we got his favorite cake!

B PAIR WORK Compare your information with a partner.

INTERCHANGE 9 Cause and effect

A Read the questions on the cards. Check (✓) the box for your opinion.

1. If teens work part-time, they won't do well in school.
   - ☐ I agree.
   - ☐ I don't agree.
   - ☐ It depends.

2. If kids play violent video games, they will become violent themselves.
   - ☐ I agree.
   - ☐ I don't agree.
   - ☐ It depends.

3. If people decrease their screen time, they'll talk more with their families.
   - ☐ I agree.
   - ☐ I don't agree.
   - ☐ It depends.

4. If a woman gets married very early, she won't invest time in her career.
   - ☐ I agree.
   - ☐ I don't agree.
   - ☐ It depends.

5. If a woman works outside the home, her children won't be happy.
   - ☐ I agree.
   - ☐ I don't agree.
   - ☐ It depends.

6. If a child has brothers and sisters, he or she won't ever feel lonely.
   - ☐ I agree.
   - ☐ I don't agree.
   - ☐ It depends.

7. If you have too many online friends, you'll have fewer "real" friends.
   - ☐ I agree.
   - ☐ I don't agree.
   - ☐ It depends.

8. If there is a heavy fine for littering, our streets will be much cleaner.
   - ☐ I agree.
   - ☐ I don't agree.
   - ☐ It depends.

9. If people work only two days a week, their lives will improve.
   - ☐ I agree.
   - ☐ I don't agree.
   - ☐ It depends.

10. If teens have a lot of freedom, they will get in trouble more often.
    - ☐ I agree.
    - ☐ I don't agree.
    - ☐ It depends.

B **GROUP WORK** Compare your opinions. Be prepared to give reasons for your opinions.

A: I think if teens work part-time, they won't do well in school.
B: I don't really agree.
C: Why not?
B: If they work part-time, they'll become more responsible. That's a positive consequence.

INTERCHANGE 10 You're hired.

A PAIR WORK Look at the following job description. Write an ad for your ideal job.

JOB FINDER   About   Careers   Education   Job search

Activities Director

Requirements:
Experience working with tourists
A "people person"
Outgoing and creative personality

Responsibilities:
Organize all leisure activities on a popular cruise ship, including planning daily tours, special onboard activities, and nightly entertainment

B PAIR WORK Take turns interviewing your classmates for the job you have created. Get as much information as you can to find the right person for the job.

useful questions

What kind of degree do you have?
What work experience do you have?
What hours can you work?
Do you mind . . . ?
Are you interested in . . . ?
Why should I hire you for the job?

C GROUP WORK Who would you hire for the job you posted? Why?

D CLASS ACTIVITY Compare the ideal jobs you created in part A. How are they similar? How are they different?

INTERCHANGE 11 True or false?

A List one movie, one TV show, one song, and one book.

B **GROUP WORK** Take turns making statements about each item. Does everyone agree with each statement?

  A: *Titanic* was filmed on a small lake in Mexico.
  B: Are you sure? Wasn't it filmed on the ocean?
  C: I'm pretty sure it was filmed in a plastic pool. I read it on the Internet.

C Now think of other famous creations and creators. Complete the chart. Make some of the items true and some false.

1. The Martian		
movie	direct	director
2. _____	was painted by	_____
painting	paint	painter
3. _____	_____	William Shakespeare
play	write	playwright
4. _____	_____	_____
song	record	singer
5. _____	_____	_____
book	write	writer
6. _____	_____	_____
invention	invent	inventor

D **GROUP WORK** Make a statement about each item to your group members. Ask them to decide which statements are true and which are false.

  A: The movie *The Martian* was directed by Steven Spielberg.
  B: I think that's true.
  C: No, that's false. It was directed by Ridley Scott. I'm sure of it.

INTERCHANGE 12 It's my life.

A **GROUP WORK** Play the board game. Follow these instructions.

1. Use small pieces of paper with your initials on them as markers.
2. Take turns tossing a coin:

   Move two spaces.   Move one space.

   Heads   **Tails**

3. Complete the sentence in the space you land on. Others ask two follow-up questions to get more information.

A: When I was little, I lived on the coast.
B: Oh, really? Did you go to the beach every day?
A: No, we only went to the beach on weekends.
C: Did you enjoy living there?

ALL ABOUT ME!

- When I was little, I . . .
- During middle school, I . . .
- I . . . while I . . .
- I used to admire . . .
- As a child, I used to spend my free time . . .
- When I was living in . . .
- Lately, I . . .
- Last year at this time, I . . .
- For the last six months, I . . .
- Free Space – Take a break!
- For the past few years, I . . .
- Many years ago, I . . .
- I have never visited . . .
- While I was . . .
- If I make a lot of money, I . . .
- I wish I . . .

FINISH

B **CLASS ACTIVITY** Tell the class an interesting fact that you learned about someone in your group.

"For the last six months, Marcia has been taking dance classes."

INTERCHANGE 13 It was hilarious!

A Complete the questionnaire.

What is the name of a TV show or movie . . . ?

1. that made you laugh a lot
2. that made you feel sad
3. that you have seen more than once
4. which had great music
5. that was about a silly story

What is the name of a TV or movie star . . . ?

6. who is very talented
7. who is famous but not very talented
8. who does things to help society
9. who is an excellent comedian
10. that reminds you of someone you know

B **PAIR WORK** Compare your questionnaires. Ask follow-up questions of your own.

A: What's the name of a TV show or movie that made you laugh a lot?
B: *Grown Ups 2.*
A: Really? Why?
B: I thought the movie was hilarious.
A: Who was in it?
B: Adam Sandler. I always enjoy his movies.
A: Well, I liked his earlier movies better.

INTERCHANGE 14 Casual observers

A PAIR WORK Look at this scene of an airport. What do you think is happening in each of the situations? Look at people's body language for clues.

A: Why do you think the couple in situation 1 looks upset?
B: Well, they might be having a fight. They look . . .
A: Who do you think the woman in situation 6 is?
B: She must be famous. She might . . .

B GROUP WORK Compare your interpretations. Do you agree or disagree?

128 Interchange 14

INTERCHANGE 16A Just a bunch of excuses

Student A

A PAIR WORK You and your partner want to get together. Ask and answer questions to find a day when you are both free. You also want to keep time open for other friends, so give excuses for those days. Write your partner's excuses on the calendar.

A: Do you want to meet on the 2nd?
B: I'm sorry. I'm going to an engagement party. Are you free on the 1st?
A: Well, I . . .

September

Sunday	Monday	Tuesday	Wednesday	Thursday	Friday	Saturday
					1 dinner with Pat	2
3	4 class	5	6	7 You want to keep this date free. Make an excuse.	8 party at Sam's	9
10	11 You want to keep this date free. Make an excuse.	12 bowling with Chris	13	14 movie with Haru	15	16
17 dinner with office friends	18 class	19	20	21 study for tomorrow's exam	22 You want to keep this date free. Make an excuse.	23
24	25	26 You want to keep these dates free. Make excuses.	27	28 dinner for Dad's birthday	29 go dancing with Jess & Bo	30 You might have a date. Give an excuse.

B PAIR WORK Now work with another student. Discuss the excuses your partner gave you in Part A. Decide which excuses were probably true and which ones were probably not true.

A: Pablo said that on the 7th he had to take care of his neighbors' cats. That was probably not true.
B: I agree. I think . . .

INTERCHANGE 15 Tough choices

A What would you do in each of these situations? Circle **a**, **b**, or **c**.
If you think you would do something else, write your suggestion next to **d**.

1. If I saw someone shoplifting in a store, I would . . .
   a. pretend I didn't notice.
   b. talk to the store manager.
   c. talk to the shoplifter.
   d. _____.

2. If I saw an elderly woman trying to cross a street, I would . . .
   a. keep walking.
   b. offer to help.
   c. try to stop traffic for her.
   d. _____.

3. If I saw someone standing on a highway next to a car with smoke coming from the engine, I would . . .
   a. continue driving.
   b. stop and help.
   c. use my cell phone to call the police.
   d. _____.

4. If I saw my friend's boyfriend or girlfriend with someone other than my friend, I would . . .
   a. say nothing.
   b. talk to my friend.
   c. talk to my friend's boyfriend or girlfriend.
   d. _____.

5. If I were eating dinner in a restaurant and I found a hair in my food, I would . . .
   a. remove it and continue eating.
   b. mention it to the server.
   c. demand to speak to the manager.
   d. _____.

B **GROUP WORK** Compare your choices for each situation in part A.

   A: What would you do if you saw someone shoplifting in a store?
   B: I'm not sure. Maybe I would pretend I didn't notice.
   C: Really? I wouldn't. I would . . .

C **CLASS ACTIVITY** Take a class survey. Find out which choice was most popular for each situation. Talk about any other suggestions people added for **d**.

INTERCHANGE 16B Just a bunch of excuses

Student B

A PAIR WORK You and your partner want to get together. Ask and answer questions to find a day when you are both free. You also want to keep time open for other friends, so give excuses for those days. Write your partner's excuses on the calendar.

A: Do you want to meet on the 2nd?
B: I'm sorry. I'm going to an engagement party. Are you free on the 1st?
A: Well, I . . .

September

Sunday	Monday	Tuesday	Wednesday	Thursday	Friday	Saturday
					1	2 Kelly's engagement party
3 You want to keep this date free. Make an excuse.	4 movie with Alex	5	6 You want to keep these dates free. Make excuses.	7	8	9
10 visit Mom and Dad	11 office party	12	13 photography workshop at school	14	15 You want to keep these dates free. Make excuses.	16
17 visit Grandma	18	19 jogging with Andie	20	21	22 party at Cameron's	23 dinner with Farah
24 family get-together	25 You need a break. Make an excuse.	26 study group meeting	27	28 work late: big report due Friday	29	30

B PAIR WORK Now work with another student. Discuss the excuses your partner gave you in Part A. Decide which excuses were probably true and which ones were probably not true.

A: Maria said that on the 9th she had to help her brother paint his kitchen. That might be true.
B: I agree. I think . . .

Grammar plus

UNIT 1

1 Past tense — page 3

> ■ Use a form of *be* with *born*: I **was born** here. (NOT: I born here.) Don't use a form of *be* with the verb *die*: He **died** last year. (NOT: He was died last year.)

Complete the conversation.

1. **A:** Do you live around here?
   B: No, I don't. I'm from Costa Rica.
   A: Really? _Were you born_ in Costa Rica?
   B: No. Actually, I was born in San Miguelito, Panama.
2. **A:** That's interesting. So where _____?
   B: I grew up in Costa Rica. My family moved there when I was little.
3. **A:** _____ in the capital?
   B: No, my family didn't live in a city. We lived in a small town called Puerto Viejo.
4. **A:** _____ away from Puerto Viejo?
   B: Oh, about eight years ago. I left Puerto Viejo to go to college.
5. **A:** Where _____ to college?
   B: I went to college in San Jose, and I live there now.
6. **A:** And _____ to Miami?
   B: I got here a few days ago. I'm visiting my cousin.

2 Used to — page 5

> ■ Use the base form of *used to* in questions and negative statements: Did you **use to** play sports? (NOT: Did you used to play sports?) I didn't **use to** like bananas. (NOT: I didn't used to like bananas.)
> ■ Don't use *never* in negative statements: I **never used to** wear sunglasses. (NOT: I never didn't use to wear sunglasses.)

Complete the conversations with the correct form of *used to*.

1. **A:** Hey, Dad. What kinds of clothes _did you use to_ wear – you know, when you were a kid?
   B: Oh, we _____ wear jeans and T-shirts – like you kids do now.
   A: Really? _____ Mom _____ dress like that, too?
   B: No, not really. She never _____ like wearing pants. She always _____ wear skirts and dresses.
2. **A:** _____ you _____ play a sport when you were a kid?
   B: Well, I _____ be a swimmer. My sister and I _____ swim on a team.
   A: Wow, that's cool! Were you good?
   B: Yeah. I _____ win gold medals all the time. And my sister _____ be the fastest swimmer on the team.

UNIT 2

1 Expressions of quantity — page 9

■ Count nouns have a plural form that usually ends in -s. Noncount nouns don't have a plural form because you can't separate and count them: Are there any **parking garages** around here? BUT Is there any **parking** around here? (NOT: Are there any parkings around here?)

Complete the conversations with the correct words in parentheses.

1. **A:** There's _____ (too many / too much) traffic in this city. There should be _____ (fewer / less) cars downtown.
   B: The problem is there _____ (aren't / isn't) enough public transportation.
   A: You're right. We should have more _____ (bus / buses). There _____ (aren't / isn't) enough of them during rush hour.

2. **A:** How do you like your new neighborhood?
   B: It's terrible, actually. There's _____ (too many / too much) noise and _____ (too few / too little) parking.
   A: That's too bad. There _____ (aren't / isn't) enough parking spaces in my neighborhood either.

3. **A:** Did you hear about the changes to the city center? Starting next month, there will be more bicycle _____ (lane / lanes) and _____ (fewer / less) street parking.
   B: That's good. There _____ (are too many / is too much) pollution downtown. I'm sure there will be _____ (fewer / less) accidents, too.
   A: That's true.

2 Indirect questions from Wh-questions — page 11

■ Indirect questions are often polite requests for information. *Can you tell me how much this magazine costs?* sounds more polite than *How much does this magazine cost?*

Complete the conversation with indirect questions.

1. **A:** Excuse me. Can you <u>tell me where the post office is</u>?
   B: Yes, of course. The post office is on the next corner.
2. **A:** And could you _____?
   B: You can find a really good restaurant on Central Avenue.
3. **A:** OK. Do you _____?
   B: Yes. The restaurant is called Giorgio's.
4. **A:** Thanks. Can you _____?
   B: Yes. They serve Italian food.
5. **A:** Oh, good! Do you _____?
   B: It opens at 5:00. Tell them Joe sent you!
   A: OK, Joe. Thanks for everything! Bye now.

Unit 2 Grammar plus **133**

UNIT 3

1 Evaluations and comparisons — page 17

> - In evaluations, *enough* goes after adjectives and before nouns.
> - adjective + *enough*: This house isn't **bright enough**. (NOT: This house isn't ~~enough bright~~.)
> - noun + *enough*: This house doesn't have **enough light**. (NOT: This house doesn't have ~~light enough~~.)

A Read each situation. Then write two sentences describing the problem, one sentence with *not . . . enough* and one with *too*.

1. Our family needs a big house. This house is very small.
   a. This house isn't big enough for us.
   b. This house is too small for us.

2. We want to live on a quiet street. This street is very noisy.
   a. _____
   b. _____

3. We need three bedrooms. This house has only two.
   a. _____
   b. _____

4. We want a spacious living room. This one is cramped.
   a. _____
   b. _____

B Rewrite the comparisons using *as . . . as*. Use *just* when possible.

1. My new apartment is smaller than my old one.
   My new apartment isn't as large as my old one.

2. This neighborhood is safer than my old one.
   _____

3. This apartment has a lot of privacy. My old one did, too.
   _____

4. My rent is reasonable now. It was very high before.
   _____

2 Wish — page 20

> - Use *could* (the past of *can*) and *would* (the past of *will*) with *wish*: I **can't** move right now, but I wish I **could**. My landlord **won't** paint my apartment, but I wish he **would**.

Match the problems with the wishes.

1. My house isn't very nice.   _c_
2. It costs a lot to live here.   ___
3. My landlord won't call me back.   ___
4. I have noisy neighbors.   ___
5. I don't like living alone.   ___
6. The buses don't run very often.   ___

a. I wish I could find a good roommate.
b. I wish he'd return my calls.
c. I wish it were more attractive.
d. I wish I could afford a car.
e. I wish their music weren't so loud.
f. I wish it weren't so expensive.

UNIT 4

1 Simple past vs. present perfect — page 23

■ Use the simple past – not the present perfect – when you say when an event ended:
I had sushi last night. (NOT: I've had sushi last night.)

Complete the conversations. Choose the best forms.

1. **A:** What _____ (did you have / have you had) for dinner last night?
   B: I _____ (tried / have tried) Indian food for the first time. _____ (Did you ever have / Have you ever had) it?
   A: A friend and I _____ (ate / have eaten) at an Indian restaurant just last week. It _____ (was / has been) delicious!

2. **A:** _____ (Did you ever take / Have you ever taken) a cooking class?
   B: No, I _____ (didn't / haven't). How about you?
   A: I _____ (took / have taken) a few classes. My last class _____ (was / has been) in December. We _____ (learned / have learned) how to make some wonderful Spanish dishes.

3. **A:** I _____ (watched / have watched) a great cooking show on TV yesterday.
   B: Really? I _____ (never saw / have never seen) a cooking show. _____ (Was it / Has it been) boring?
   A: No, it _____ (wasn't / hasn't). It _____ (was / has been) very interesting!

2 Sequence adverbs — page 25

■ *Then, next,* and *after that* mean the same. *First* comes first, and *finally* comes last; you can use the other adverbs in any order: **First,** put some water in a pan. **Then/Next/After that,** put the eggs in the water. **Finally,** boil the eggs for 7 minutes.

Unscramble the steps in this recipe for hamburgers. Then write the steps in order.

salt and pepper   add   in the bowl   to the meat   then

_____ : _____

2 pounds of chopped beef   put in a bowl   first,

Step 1 : _First, put 2 pounds of chopped beef in a bowl._

put   the burgers   in a pan   finally,   and cook for 10 minutes

_____ : _____

next,   the meat   and the salt and pepper   mix   together

_____ : _____

into four burgers   after that,   with your hands   form the meat

_____ : _____

UNIT 5

1 Future with *be going to* and *will* page 31

> - Use the base form of the verb – not the infinitive (*to* + base form) – with *will*:
>   I think I**'ll go** to Hawaii next winter. (NOT: I think I'll to go to Hawaii next winter.)
> - Use *be going to* – not *will* – when you know something is going to happen:
>   Look at those black clouds. It**'s going to** rain. (NOT: It will rain.)

Complete the conversation with the correct form of *be going to* or *will* and the verbs in parentheses.

A: It's Friday – at last! What _are you going to do_ (do) this weekend?
B: I'm not sure. I'm really tired, so I probably _____ (not do) anything exciting. Maybe I _____ (see) a movie on Saturday. How about you? How _____ (spend) your weekend?
A: My wife and I _____ (do) some work on our house. We _____ (paint) the living room on Saturday. On Sunday, we _____ (clean) all the rugs.
B: _____ (do) anything fun?
A: Oh, I think we _____ (have) a lot of fun. We like working around the house. And Sunday's my birthday, so we _____ (have) dinner at my favorite Italian restaurant.
B: Now that sounds like fun!

2 Modals for necessity and suggestion page 33

> - Some modals for necessity and suggestion are stronger than others.
>   Weak (for advice or an opinion): *should, ought to*
>   Stronger (for a warning): *had better*
>   Strongest (for an obligation): *must, need to, have to*

Choose the correct word or words to complete the advice to travelers.

1. You _____ (must / should) show identification at the airport. They won't allow you on a plane without an official ID.
2. Your ID _____ (needs to / ought to) have a picture of you on it. It's required.
3. The picture of you _____ (has to / ought to) be recent. They won't accept an old photo.
4. Travelers _____ (must / should) get to the airport at least two hours before their flight. It's not a good idea to get there later than that.
5. All travelers _____ (have to / had better) go through airport security. It's necessary for passenger safety.
6. Many airlines don't serve food, so passengers on long flights probably _____ (must / ought to) buy something to eat at the airport.

UNIT 6

1 Two-part verbs; *will* for responding to requests — page 37

- Two-part verbs are verb + particle.
- If the object of a two-part verb is a noun, the noun can come before or after the particle: **Take out** the trash./**Take** the trash **out**.
- If the object is a pronoun, the pronoun must come before the particle: **Take** it **out**. (NOT: Take ~~out it~~.)

Write conversations. First, rewrite the request given by changing the position of the particle. Then write a response to the request using *it* or *them*.

1. Put away your clothes, please.
   A: Put your clothes away, please.
   B: OK. I'll put them away.

2. Turn the lights on, please.
   A: _____
   B: _____

3. Please turn your music down.
   A: _____
   B: _____

4. Clean up the kitchen, please.
   A: _____
   B: _____

5. Turn off your phone, please.
   A: _____
   B: _____

2 Requests with modals and *Would you mind . . . ?* — page 39

- Use the base form of the verb – not the infinitive (*to* + base form) – with the modals *can*, *could*, and *would*: **Could** you **get** me a sandwich? (NOT: Could you ~~to~~ get me a sandwich?)
- Requests with modals and *Would you mind . . . ?* are polite – even without *please*. *Can you get me a sandwich?* sounds much more polite than *Get me a sandwich*.

Change these sentences to polite requests. Use the words in parentheses.

1. Bring in the mail. (could)
   Could you bring in the mail?

2. Put your shoes by the door. (would you mind)
   _____

3. Don't leave dishes in the sink. (would you mind)
   _____

4. Change the TV channel. (can)
   _____

5. Don't play ball inside. (would you mind)
   _____

6. Clean up your mess. (would you mind)
   _____

7. Put away the clean towels. (can)
   _____

8. Pick up your things. (could)
   _____

Unit 6 Grammar plus

UNIT 7

1 Infinitives and gerunds for uses and purposes — page 45

> - Sentences with infinitives and gerunds mean the same: *I use my cell phone to send text messages* means the same as *I use my cell phone for sending text messages*.
> - Use a gerund – not an infinitive – after *for*: *Satellites are used **for studying** weather.* (NOT: *Satellites are used for ~~to study~~ weather*.)

Read each sentence about a technology item. Write two sentences about the item's use and purpose. Use the information in parentheses.

1. My sister's car has a built-in GPS system. (She use / get directions)
   a. <u>She uses the GPS system to get directions.</u>
   b. <u>She uses the GPS system for getting directions.</u>
2. I love my new smartphone. (I use / take pictures)
   a. _____
   b. _____
3. That's a flash drive. (You use / back up files)
   a. _____
   b. _____
4. My little brother wants his own laptop. (He would only use / watch movies and play games)
   a. _____
   b. _____
5. I'm often on my computer all day long. (I use / shop online and do research)
   a. _____
   b. _____

2 Imperatives and infinitives for giving suggestions — page 47

> - With imperatives and infinitives, *not* goes before – not after – *to*: *Try **not to** talk too long.* (NOT: *Try ~~to not~~ talk too long*.)

Rewrite the sentences as suggestions. Use the words in parentheses.

1. When you go to the movies, turn off your phone. (don't forget)
   <u>When you go to the movies, don't forget to turn off your phone.</u>
2. Don't talk on the phone when you're in an elevator. (try)
   _____
3. Don't eat or drink anything when you're at the computer. (be sure)
   _____
4. Clean your computer screen and keyboard once a week. (remember)
   _____
5. Don't use your tablet outside when it's raining. (make sure)
   _____
6. When the bell rings to start class, put your music player away! (be sure)
   _____

UNIT 8

1 Relative clauses of time — page 51

- Relative clauses with *when* describe the word *time* or a noun that refers to a period of time, such as *day, night, month,* and *year.*

Combine the two sentences using *when.*

1. Thanksgiving is a holiday. Entire families get together.
   Thanksgiving is a holiday when entire families get together.
2. It's a wonderful time. People give thanks for the good things in their lives.

3. It's a day. Everyone eats much more than usual.

4. I remember one particular year. The whole family came to our house.

5. That year was very cold. It snowed all Thanksgiving day.

6. I remember another thing about that Thanksgiving. My brother and I baked eight pies.

2 Adverbial clauses of time — page 54

- An adverbial clause of time can come before or after the main clause. When it comes before the main clause, use a comma. When it comes after the main clause, don't use a comma: When Ginny and Tom met, they both lived in San Juan. BUT: Ginny and Tom met when they both lived in San Juan.
- The words *couple* and *family* are collective nouns. They are usually used with singular verbs: When a couple **gets** married, they often receive gifts. (NOT: When a couple ~~get~~ married, they often receive gifts.)

Combine the two sentences using the adverb in parentheses. Write one sentence with the adverbial clause before the main clause and another with the adverbial clause after the main clause.

1. Students complete their courses. A school holds a graduation ceremony. (after)
   a. After students complete their courses, a school holds a graduation ceremony.
   b. A school holds a graduation ceremony after students complete their courses.
2. Students gather to put on robes and special hats. The ceremony starts. (before)
   a.
   b.
3. Music plays. The students walk in a line to their seats. (when)
   a.
   b.
4. School officials and teachers make speeches. Students get their diplomas. (after)
   a.
   b.
5. The ceremony is finished. Students throw their hats into the air and cheer. (when)
   a.
   b.

UNIT 9

1 Time contrasts /page 59/

> ■ Use the modal *might* to say something is possible in the present or future: In a few years, movie theaters **might** not exist. = In a few years, maybe movie theaters won't exist.

Complete the conversation with the correct form of the verbs in parentheses. Use the past, present, or future tense.

A: I saw a fascinating program last night. It talked about the past, the present, and the future.
B: What kinds of things did it describe?
A: Well, for example, the normal work week in the 19th century _____ (be) over 60 hours. Nowadays, many people _____ (work) around 40 hours a week.
B: Well, that sounds like progress.
A: You're right. But on the show, they said that most people _____ (work) fewer hours in the future. They also talked about the way we shop. These days, many of us _____ (shop) online. In the old days, there _____ (be) no supermarkets, so people _____ (have to) go to a lot of different stores. In the future, people _____ (do) all their shopping from their phones.
B: I don't believe that.
A: Me neither. What about cars? Do you think people _____ (still drive) cars a hundred years from now?
B: What did they say on the show?
A: They said that before the car, people _____ (walk) everywhere. Nowadays, we _____ (drive) everywhere. And that _____ (not change).

2 Conditional sentences with *if* clauses /page 61/

> ■ The *if* clause can come before or after the main clause: **If** I change my eating habits, I'll feel healthier./I'll feel healthier **if** I change my eating habits. Always use a comma when the *if* clause comes before the main clause.
> ■ For the future of *can*, use *will be able to*: If you save some money, you**'ll be able to buy** a car. (NOT: . . . you'll can buy a car.)
> ■ For the future of *must*, use *will have to*: If you get a dog, you**'ll have to take care** of it. (NOT: . . . you'll must take care of it.)

Complete the sentences with the correct form of the verbs in parentheses.

1. If you ____exercise____ (exercise) more often, you'__ll feel__ (feel) more energetic.
2. If you _____ (join) a gym, exercise _____ (become) part of your routine.
3. You _____ (not have to) worry about staying in shape if you _____ (work out) three or four times a week.
4. If you _____ (ride) a bike or _____ (run) a few times a week, you _____ (lose) weight and _____ (gain) muscle.
5. You _____ (sleep) better at night if you _____ (exercise) regularly.
6. If you _____ (start) exercising, you _____ (might/not have) as many colds and other health problems.

140 Unit 9 Grammar plus

UNIT 10

1 Gerunds; short responses — page 65

■ Short responses with *so* and *neither* are ways of agreeing. The subject (noun or pronoun) comes after the verb: I love traveling. So **do I**. (NOT: So ~~I do~~.) I can't stand talking on the phone. Neither **can I**. (NOT: Neither ~~I can~~.)

Rewrite A's line using the words given. Then write an agreement for B.

1. I hate working alone. (can't stand)
   A: I can't stand working alone.
   B: Neither can I.
2. I don't like reading about politics or politicians. (interested in)
   A: _____
   B: _____
3. I can solve problems. (good at)
   A: _____
   B: _____
4. I have no problem with working on weekends. (don't mind)
   A: _____
   B: _____
5. I love learning new things. (enjoy)
   A: _____
   B: _____
6. I can't develop new ideas. (not good at)
   A: _____
   B: _____

2 Clauses with *because* — page 68

■ Clauses with *because* answer the question "Why?" or "Why not?": Why would you make a good flight attendant? I'd make a good flight attendant **because** I love traveling, and I'm good with people.

Complete the sentences with *because* and the phrases in the box.

> I don't write very well
> I love arguing with people
> I'm afraid of flying
> ✓ I'm much too short
> I'm not patient enough to work with kids
> I'm really bad with numbers

1. I could never be a fashion model because I'm much too short .
2. I wouldn't make a good high school teacher _____.
3. I wouldn't want to be a flight attendant _____.
4. I could never be an accountant _____.
5. I would make a bad journalist _____.
6. I'd be an excellent lawyer _____.

Unit 10 Grammar plus

UNIT 11

1 Passive with *by* (simple past) — page 73

- The past participle of regular verbs is the same form as the simple past: Leonardo da Vinci **painted** *Mona Lisa* in 1503. *Mona Lisa* was **painted** by Leonardo da Vinci in 1503.
- The past participle of some – but not all – irregular verbs is the same form as the simple past: The Egyptians **built** the Pyramids. The Pyramids were **built** by the Egyptians. BUT Jane Austen **wrote** *Pride and Prejudice*. *Pride and Prejudice* was **written** by Jane Austen.

Change the sentences from active to passive with *by*.

1. The Chinese invented paper around 100 C.E.
   Paper was invented by the Chinese around 100 C.E.
2. Marie Curie discovered radium in 1898.
   _____
3. Dr. Felix Hoffmann made the first aspirin in 1899.
   _____
4. Tim Berners-Lee developed the World Wide Web in 1989.
   _____
5. William Herschel identified the planet Uranus in 1781.
   _____
6. Georges Bizet wrote the opera *Carmen* in the 1870s.
   _____

2 Passive without *by* (simple present) — page 75

- When it is obvious or not important who is doing the action, don't use a *by* phrase: Both the Olympics and the World Cup are held every four years. (NOT: . . . are held ~~by people~~ . . .)

Complete the information with *is* or *are* and the past participle of the verbs in the box.

base	know
export	✓ speak
import	use

1. Portuguese – not Spanish – *is spoken* in Brazil.
2. Diamonds and gold from South Africa _____ by countries all over the world.
3. The U.S. dollar _____ in Puerto Rico.
4. Colombia _____ for its delicious coffee.
5. Many electronic products _____ by Japan and South Korea. It's an important industry for these two countries.
6. The economy in many island countries, such as Jamaica, _____ on tourism.

UNIT 12

1 Past continuous vs. simple past — page 79

> ■ When the past continuous is used with the simple past, both actions happened at the same time, but the past continuous action started earlier. The simple past action interrupted the past continuous action.
>
> Earlier action — 6:00 — I was watching TV
> Later action — 6:20 — when the phone rang.

Complete the conversations with the correct form of the verbs in parentheses. Use the past continuous or the simple past.

1. **A:** What happened to you?
   B: I _____fell_____ (fall) while I _____was jogging_____ (jog) in the park.
2. **A:** _____ you _____ (see) the storm yesterday?
   B: Yes! It _____ (start) while I _____ (drive) to work.
3. **A:** We finally _____ (move) to a larger apartment.
   B: That's good. I know you _____ (live) in a tiny place when your daughter _____ (be) born.
4. **A:** My sister _____ (have) a bad accident. She _____ (hurt) her back when she _____ (lift) weights at the gym.
   B: That _____ (happen) to me last year, but I _____ (not lift) weights. I _____ (take) a boxing class, and I _____ (trip).

2 Present perfect continuous — page 81

> ■ The same time expressions used with the present perfect can also be used with the present perfect continuous. Don't confuse *for* and *since*: I've been working here **for** 5 years./I've been working here **since** 2010.

Complete the sentences with the present perfect continuous form of the verbs in parentheses.

1. **A:** What _____have_____ you _____been doing_____ all day?
   B: I _____ (clean) the house, and Peter _____ (watch) TV. He _____ (not feel) very well lately.
   A: How _____ you _____ (feel) these days?
   B: I _____ (feel) great. I _____ (not eat) any junk food, and I _____ (exercise) a lot. I _____ (take) really good care of myself.
2. **A:** How long _____ you and Joe _____ (date)?
   B: We _____ (go out) together for almost a year. Can you believe it?
   A: Maya and I _____ (date) for even longer. I think it's time to get married. We _____ (talk) about it a lot lately.
   B: Joe and I _____ (not talk) about marriage, but I _____ (think) about it.

Unit 12 Grammar plus

UNIT 13

1 Participles as adjectives — page 87

> Adjectives ending in *–ing* are present participles. They are things that *cause* a feeling.
> Adjectives ending in *–ed* are past participles. They *express* the feeling.

Complete the sentences with the correct participle.

1. Why are we watching this _____boring_____ movie? Aren't you _____bored_____ with it? (boring / bored)
2. Kristen Stewart is an _____ actress. I'm _____ by her talent. (amazing / amazed)
3. Are you _____ in computer-generated special effects? The latest 3-D movies are very _____. (interesting / interested)
4. I had an _____ experience the last time I went to the movies. I started to cough, and I couldn't stop. I was really _____. (embarrassing / embarrassed)
5. Julie and I saw an Italian comedy yesterday. I found it _____, but Julie didn't seem very _____ by it. (amusing / amused)
6. Oh, I'm really _____ with Jeremy right now. He took me to the most _____ movie last night. I wanted to walk out after half an hour, but he wouldn't leave! (disgusting / disgusted)
7. Do you think sci-fi movie directors make their films _____ intentionally? I get so _____ by the complicated storylines and weird characters. (confusing / confused)
8. I think that great books make great movies. If I find a book _____, I'm usually _____ by the movie, too. (fascinating / fascinated)

2 Relative pronouns for people and things — page 89

> Relative clauses give information about nouns. Don't use a personal pronoun in a relative clause: He's an actor **that** won two Oscars. (NOT: He's an actor that he won two Oscars.)

Complete the conversations. Use *that* for things and *who* for people.

A: How did you like the movie last night? Was it any good?
B: It wasn't bad, but it's not the kind of movie _____that_____ makes you think. I like films _____ have a strong message and interesting storylines.
A: How about the acting? Did you like the actors _____ star in it?
B: Jessica Biel is pretty good, actually.
A: Oh, she's that beautiful actress _____ is married to Justin Timberlake.
B: Justin who? Who's that?
A: Oh, you know him. He's the one _____ was in the band 'NSync years ago. It was a "boy band" _____ was popular in the 1990s.
B: I remember 'NSync, but I don't remember the names of the guys _____ were in the band.
A: Well, I loved Justin Timberlake when I was a kid. And he's not a bad actor. Did you see the movie *The Social Network*?
B: I did see that. It's about the guys _____ started Facebook, right? I didn't realize Justin Timberlake was in it. Now I'll have to see it again!

UNIT 14

1 Modals and adverbs — page 93

> ■ Use the modals *might/may*, *could*, and *must* and the adverbs *maybe/perhaps*, *probably*, and *definitely* when you aren't sure about what you're saying:
> Slight possibility: *might, may, maybe, perhaps*
> Possibility: *could, probably*
> Strong possibility: *must, definitely*

Rewrite each sentence in different ways, using the words in parentheses.

1. Perhaps it means she doesn't agree with you.
   a. (maybe) _Maybe it means she doesn't agree with you._
   b. (might) _____
   c. (may) _____
2. That gesture could mean, "Come here."
   a. (probably) _____
3. That almost definitely means he doesn't understand you.
   a. (must) _____

2 Permission, obligation, and prohibition — page 95

> ■ Use *have/has* with *got to*: You**'ve got to** keep the door closed. (NOT: You ~~got to~~ keep the door closed.)

Complete the conversations with the words and phrases in the box.
Use each word or phrase only once.

are allowed to	✓ can't
aren't allowed to	have to
can	have got to

1. **A:** Oh, no! That sign says, "No fishing." That means we _____ *can't* _____ fish here.
   B: You're right. We _____ go somewhere else to fish. I think you _____ fish in the pond on Cedar Road. Let's go there.
2. **A:** What does that sign mean?
   B: It means bad news for us. It means you _____ bring dogs to the beach. We'd better take Buddy home.
3. **A:** Please don't leave your garbage here. You _____ put it in the trash room down the hall. That's one of the building's rules.
   B: I'm really sorry.
4. **A:** You _____ put your bike in the bike room downstairs, if you want. It's much safer than locking it up outside.
   B: Oh, that's great! I'll do that. I didn't know about the bike room.

UNIT 15

1 Unreal conditional sentences with if clauses — page 101

> ■ The clauses in unreal conditional sentences can come in either order. Don't use a comma when the *if* clause comes second: **If** I won the lottery, I'd share the money with my family./I'd share the money with my family **if** I won the lottery.

Complete the conversation with the correct form of the verbs in parentheses.

1. **A:** If a friend _____ (ask) to borrow some money, what _____ you _____ (say)?
   B: Well, if I _____ (have) any extra money that month, I _____ probably _____ (give) it to her.

2. **A:** What _____ you _____ (do) if someone _____ (give) you a million dollars?
   B: Hmm, I'm not sure. I _____ (buy) a lot of nice clothes and jewelry, or I _____ (spend) some and _____ (give) some away, or I _____ (put) it all in the bank.

3. **A:** If you _____ (think) a friend was doing something dangerous, _____ you _____ (say) something to him, or _____ you _____ (keep) quiet?
   B: I _____ definitely _____ (talk) to my friend about it.

4. **A:** What _____ you _____ (do) if you _____ (have) a problem with your boss?
   B: That's a hard one. If that _____ (happen), I _____ (talk) to the human resources department about it, or I _____ just _____ (sit down) with my boss and _____ (talk) about the situation.

2 Past modals — page 103

> ■ Use *should have* and *would have* for all subjects. They don't change form: He **should have called** sooner. (NOT: He should has called sooner.)

Read the situations. Use the words in parentheses to write opinions and suggestions.

1. My neighbor had a party last night. It was very loud, so I called the police.
   (you / speak / to your neighbor first)
   You should have spoken to your neighbor first.

2. The mail carrier put someone else's mail in my box. I threw it away.
   (you / write / a note and leave / the mail in your box)
   _____

3. My sister asked if I liked her new dress. It didn't look good on her, but I said it did.
   (I / tell her the truth)
   _____

4. A salesperson called me last night. I didn't want to buy anything, but I let her talk to me for almost half an hour.
   (I / tell her I'm not interested / hang up)
   _____

UNIT 16

1 Reported speech: requests — page 107

- When a reported request is negative, *not* comes before *to*: Don't leave your wet towel on the floor. She told me **not to leave** my wet towel on the floor.
(NOT: She told me to not leave my wet towel on the floor.)

Harry's roommate, Tyler, is making some requests. Read what Tyler said to Harry. Write the requests with the verbs in parentheses and reported speech.

1. "Can you put away your clean clothes?" (ask)
   Tyler asked Harry to put away his clean clothes.

2. "Meet me in the cafeteria at school at noon." (say)

3. "Don't leave your shoes in the living room." (tell)

4. "Hang up your wet towels." (say)

5. "Could you stop using my phone?" (ask)

6. "Make your bed on weekdays." (tell)

7. "Don't eat my food." (say)

8. "Be a better roommate!" (tell)

2 Reported speech: statements — page 109

- The tense of the introducing verb (*ask, say, tell*) changes when the sentence is reported: simple present → simple past; present continuous → past continuous; present perfect → past perfect. Modals change, too: *can* → *could*; *will* → *would*; *may* → *might*.

Bill and Kathy are having a barbecue on Sunday. They're upset because a lot of their friends can't come. Read what their friends said. Change the excuses into reported speech.

1. Lori: "I have to visit my grandparents that day."
   Lori said that she had to visit her grandparents that day.

2. Mario: "I'm going to a play on Sunday."

3. Julia: "I've promised to take my brother to the movies that day."

4. Daniel: "I can't come. I have to study for a huge exam on Monday."

5. The neighbors: "We'll be out of town all weekend."

6. Alice: "I may have to babysit my nephew."

Grammar plus answer key

Unit 1
1 Past tense
2. did you grow up/are you from
3. Did you live
4. When did you move
5. did you go
6. when did you come/get

2 Used to
1. A: Hey, Dad. What kinds of clothes **did you use to** wear – you know, when you were a kid?
   B: Oh, we **used to** wear jeans and T-shirts – like you kids do now.
   A: Really? **Did** Mom **use to** dress like that, too?
   B: No, not really. She never **used to** like wearing pants. She always **used to** wear skirts and dresses.
2. A: **Did** you **use to** play a sport when you were a kid?
   B: Well, I **used to** be a swimmer. My sister and I **used to** swim on a team.
   A: Wow, that's cool! Were you good?
   B: Yeah. I **used to** win gold medals all the time. And my sister **used to** be the fastest swimmer on the team.

Unit 2
1 Expressions of quantity
1. A: There's **too much** traffic in this city. There should be **fewer** cars downtown.
   B: The problem is there **isn't** enough public transportation.
   A: You're right. We should have more **buses**. There **aren't** enough of them during rush hour.
2. A: How do you like your new neighborhood?
   B: It's terrible, actually. There's **too much** noise and **too little** parking.
   A: That's too bad. There **aren't** enough parking spaces in my neighborhood either.
3. A: Did you hear about the changes to the city center? Starting next month, there will be more bicycle **lanes** and **less** street parking.
   B: That's good. There **is too much** pollution downtown. I'm sure there will be **fewer** accidents, too.
   A: That's true.

2 Indirect questions from Wh-questions
Answers may vary. Some possible answers:
2. And could you **tell me where I can find a good restaurant**?
3. Do you **know what the name of the restaurant is**?
4. Can you **tell me what type of food they serve**?
5. Do you **know what time the restaurant opens**?

Unit 3
1 Evaluations and comparisons
A
Answers may vary. Some possible answers:
2. This street isn't quiet enough./This street is too noisy.
3. This house doesn't have enough bedrooms./This house is too small for us./This house has too few bedrooms for us.
4. This living room isn't spacious enough./This living room doesn't have enough space./This living room is too cramped/small.

B
Answers may vary. Some possible answers:
2. My old neighborhood isn't as safe as this one.
3. This apartment has (just) as much privacy as my old one.
4. My rent isn't as high as it used to be.

2 Wish
2. f   3. b   4. e   5. a   6. d

Unit 4
1 Simple past vs. present perfect
1. A: What **did you have** for dinner last night?
   B: I **tried** Indian food for the first time. **Have you ever had** it?
   A: A friend and I **ate** at an Indian restaurant just last week. It **was** delicious!
2. A: **Have you ever taken** a cooking class?
   B: No, **I haven't**. How about you?
   A: **I have taken** a few classes. My last class **was** in December. We **learned** how to make some wonderful Spanish dishes.
3. A: I **watched** a great cooking show on TV yesterday.
   B: Really? I **have never seen** a cooking show. **Was it** boring?
   A: No, it **wasn't**. It **was** very interesting!

2 Sequence adverbs
Step 1: First, put 2 pounds of chopped beef in a bowl.
Step 2: Then add salt and pepper to the meat in the bowl.
Step 3: Next, mix the meat and the salt and pepper together.
Step 4: After that, form the meat into four burgers with your hands.
Step 5: Finally, put the burgers in a pan and cook for 10 minutes.

Unit 5
1 Future with *be going to* and *will*
B: I'm not sure. I'm really tired, so I probably **won't do** anything exciting. Maybe I'**ll see** a movie on Saturday. How about you? How **are you going to spend** your weekend?
A: My wife and I **are going to do** some work on our house. We'**re going to paint** the living room on Saturday. On Sunday, we'**re going to clean** all the rugs.
B: **Are(n't) you going to do** anything fun?
A: Oh, I think we'**ll have/'re going to have** a lot of fun. We like working around the house. And Sunday's my birthday, so we'**re going to have** dinner at my favorite Italian restaurant.
B: Now that sounds like fun!

2 Modals for necessity and suggestions
1. You **must** show identification at the airport. They won't allow you on a plane without an official ID.
2. Your ID **needs to** have a picture of you on it. It's required.
3. The picture of you **has to** be recent. They won't accept an old photo.
4. Travelers **should** get to the airport at least two hours before their flight. It's not a good idea to get there later than that.
5. All travelers **have to** go through airport security. It's necessary for passenger safety.
6. Many airlines don't serve food, so passengers on long flights probably **ought to** buy something to eat at the airport.

Unit 6
1 Two-part verbs; *will* for responding to requests
2. A: Turn on the lights, please.
   B: OK. I'll turn them on.
3. A: Please turn down your music.
   B: OK. I'll turn it down.
4. A: Clean the kitchen up, please.
   B: OK. I'll clean it up.
5. A: Turn your phone off, please.
   B: OK. I'll turn it off.

2 Requests with modals and *Would you mind . . . ?*
2. Would you mind putting your shoes by the door?
3. Would you mind not leaving dishes in the sink?
4. Can you change the TV channel?
5. Would you mind not playing ball inside?
6. Would you mind cleaning up your mess?
7. Can you put away the clean towels?
8. Could you pick up your things?

Unit 7

1 Infinitives and gerunds for uses and purposes
2. a. I use my smartphone/it to take pictures.
   b. I use my smartphone/it for taking pictures.
3. a. You use a flash drive/it to back up files.
   b. You use a flash drive/it for backing up files.
4. a. He would only use a laptop/it to watch movies and play games.
   b. He would only use a laptop/it for watching movies and playing games.
5. a. I use my computer/it to shop online and do research.
   b. I use my computer/it for shopping online and doing research.

2 Imperatives and infinitives for giving suggestions
2. Try not to talk on the phone when you're in an elevator.
3. Be sure not to eat or drink anything when you're at the computer.
4. Remember to clean your computer screen and keyboard once a week.
5. Make sure not to use your tablet outside when it's raining.
6. When the bell rings to start class, be sure to put your music player away!

Unit 8

1 Relative clauses of time
2. It's a wonderful time when people give thanks for the good things in their lives.
3. It's a day when everyone eats much more than usual.
4. I remember one particular year when the whole family came to our house.
5. That year was very cold when it snowed all Thanksgiving day.
6. I remember another thing about that Thanksgiving when my brother and I baked eight pies.

2 Adverbial clauses of time
2. a. Before the ceremony starts, students gather to put on robes and special hats.
   b. Students gather to put on robes and special hats before the ceremony starts.
3. a. When music plays, the students walk in a line to their seats.
   b. The students walk in a line to their seats when music plays.
4. a. After school officials and teachers make speeches, students get their diplomas.
   b. Students get their diplomas after school officials and teachers make speeches.
5. a. When the ceremony is finished, students throw their hats into the air and cheer.
   b. Students throw their hats into the air and cheer when the ceremony is finished.

Unit 9

1 Time contrasts
A: I saw a fascinating program last night. It talked about the past, the present, and the future.
B: What kinds of things did it describe?
A: Well, for example, the normal work week in the 19th century **was/used to be** over 60 hours. Nowadays, many people **work/are working** around 40 hours a week.
B: Well, that sounds like progress.
A: You're right. But on the show, they said that most people **will work/might work** fewer hours in the future. They also talked about the way we shop. These days, many of us **shop** online. In the old days, there **were** no supermarkets, so people **had to go/used to have to go** to a lot of different stores. In the future, people **will do/might do/are going to do** all their shopping from their phones.
B: I don't believe that.
A: Me neither. What about cars? Do you think people **will still drive/are still going to drive** cars a hundred years from now?
B: What did they say on the show?
A: They said that before the car, people **walked/used to walk** everywhere. Nowadays, we **drive** everywhere. And that **won't change/isn't going to change/'s not going to change**.

2 Conditional sentences with *if* clauses
2. If you **join** a gym, exercise **will become** part of your routine.
3. You **won't have to** worry about staying in shape if you **work out** three or four times a week.
4. If you **ride** a bike or **run** a few times a week, you**'ll lose** weight and **gain** muscle.
5. You**'ll sleep** better at night if you **exercise** regularly.
6. If you **start** exercising, you **might not have** as many colds and other health problems.

Unit 10

1 Gerunds; short responses
2. A: I'm not interested in reading about politics or politicians.
   B: Neither am I.
3. A: I'm good at solving problems.
   B: So am I.
4. A: I don't mind working on weekends.
   B: Neither do I.
5. A: I enjoy learning new things.
   B: So do I.
6. A: I'm not good at developing new ideas.
   B: Neither am I.

2 Clauses with *because*
2. I wouldn't make a good high school teacher **because I'm not patient enough to work with kids**.
3. I wouldn't want to be a flight attendant **because I'm afraid of flying**.
4. I could never be an accountant **because I'm really bad with numbers**.
5. I would make a bad journalist **because I don't write very well**.
6. I'd be an excellent lawyer **because I love arguing with people**.

Unit 11

1 Passive with *by* (simple past)
2. Radium was discovered by Marie Curie in 1898.
3. The first aspirin was made by Dr. Felix Hoffmann in 1899.
4. The World Wide Web was developed by Tim Berners-Lee in 1989.
5. The planet Uranus was identified in 1781 by William Herschel.
6. The opera *Carmen* was written by Georges Bizet in the 1870s.

2 Passive without *by* (simple present)
2. Diamonds and gold from South Africa **are imported** by countries all over the world.
3. The U.S. dollar **is used** in Puerto Rico.
4. Colombia **is known** for its delicious coffee.
5. Many electronic products **are exported** by Japan and Korea. It's an important industry for these two countries.
6. The economy in many island countries, such as Jamaica, **is based** on tourism.

Unit 12

1 Past continuous vs. simple past
2. A: **Did** you **see** the storm yesterday?
   B: Yes! It **started** while I **was driving** to work.
3. A: We finally **moved** to a larger apartment.
   B: That's good. I know you **were living** in a tiny place when your daughter **was** born.
4. A: My sister **had** a bad accident. She **hurt** her back when she **was lifting** weights at the gym.
   B: That **happened** to me last year, but I **wasn't lifting** weights. I **was taking** a boxing class, and I **tripped**.

2 Present perfect continuous
1. A: What **have** you **been doing** all day?
   B: I**'ve been cleaning** the house, and Peter **has been watching** TV. He **hasn't been feeling** very well lately.
   A: How **have** you **been feeling** these days?
   B: I**'ve been feeling** great. I **haven't been eating** any junk food, and I**'ve been exercising** a lot. I**'ve been taking** really good care of myself.

Grammar plus answer key 149

2. A: How long **have** you and Joe **been dating**?
   B: We**'ve been going out** together for almost a year. Can you believe it?
   A: Maya and I **have been dating** for even longer. I think it's time to get married. We**'ve been talking** about it a lot lately.
   B: Joe and I **haven't been talking** about marriage, but I**'ve been thinking** about it.

Unit 13

1 Participles as adjectives
2. Kristen Stewart is an **amazing** actress. I'm **amazed** by her talent.
3. Are you **interested** in computer-generated special effects? The latest 3-D movies are very **interesting**.
4. I had an **embarrassing** experience the last time I went to the movies. I started to cough, and I couldn't stop. I was really **embarrassed**.
5. Julie and I saw an Italian comedy yesterday. I found it **amusing**, but Julie didn't seem very **amused** by it.
6. Oh, I'm really **disgusted** with Jeremy right now. He took me to the most **disgusting** movie last night. I wanted to walk out after half an hour, but he wouldn't leave!
7. Do you think sci-fi movie directors make their films **confusing** intentionally? I get so **confused** by the complicated storylines and weird characters.
8. I think that great books make great movies. If I find a book **fascinating**, I'm usually **fascinated** by the movie, too.

2 Relative pronouns for people and things
A: How did you like the movie last night? Was it any good?
B: It wasn't bad, but it's not the kind of movie **that** makes you think. I like films **that** have a strong message and interesting storylines.
A: How about the acting? Did you like the actors **who** star in it?
B: Jessica Biel is pretty good, actually.
A: Oh, she's that beautiful actress **who** is married to Justin Timberlake.
B: Justin who? Who's that?
A: Oh, you know him. He's the one **who** was in the band 'NSync years ago. It was a "boy band" **that** was popular in the 1990s.
B: I remember 'NSync, but I don't remember the names of the guys **who** were in the band.
A: Well, I loved Justin Timberlake when I was a kid. And he's not a bad actor. Did you see the movie *The Social Network*?
B: I did see that. It's about the guys **who** started Facebook, right? I didn't realize Justin Timberlake was in it. Now I'll have to see it again!

Unit 14

1 Modals and adverbs
1. a. Maybe it means she doesn't agree with you.
   b. It might mean she doesn't agree with you.
   c. It may mean she doesn't agree with you.
2. a. That gesture probably means, "Come here."
3. a. That must mean he doesn't understand you.

2 Permission, obligation, and prohibition
1. A: Oh, no! That sign says, "No fishing." That means we **can't** fish here.
   B: You're right. We**'ve got to/have to** go somewhere else to fish. I think you**'re allowed to/can** fish in the pond on Cedar Road. Let's go there.
2. A: What does that sign mean?
   B: It means bad news for us. It means you **aren't allowed to** bring dogs to the beach. We'd better take Buddy home.
3. A: Please don't leave your garbage here. You**'ve got to/have to** put it in the trash room down the hall. That's one of the building's rules.
   B: I'm really sorry.
4. A: You **can** put your bike in the bike room downstairs, if you want. It's much safer than locking it up outside.
   B: Oh, that's great! I'll do that. I didn't know about the bike room.

Unit 15

1 Unreal conditional sentences with *if* clauses
1. A: If a friend **asked** to borrow some money, what **would** you **say**?
   B: Well, if I **had** any extra money that month, I **would** probably **give** it to her.
2. A: What **would/could** you **do** if someone **gave** you a million dollars?
   B: Hmm, I'm not sure. I **could/might buy** a lot of nice clothes and jewelry, or I **could/might spend** some and **give** some away, or I **could/might put** it all in the bank.
3. A: If you **thought** a friend was doing something dangerous, **would** you **say** something to him, or **would** you **keep** quiet?
   B: I **would** definitely **talk** to my friend about it.
4. A: What **would** you **do** if you **had** a problem with your boss?
   B: That's a hard one. If that **happened**, I **might/could talk** to the human resources department about it, or I **might/could** just **sit down** with my boss and **talk** about the situation.

2 Past modals
2. You should have written a note and left the mail in your box.
3. I would have told her the truth.
4. I would have told her I wasn't interested and hung up (the phone).

Unit 16

1 Reported speech: requests
2. Tyler said to meet him in the cafeteria at school at noon.
3. Tyler told him/Harry not to leave his shoes in the living room.
4. Tyler said to hang up his wet towels.
5. Tyler asked him/Harry to stop using his/Tyler's phone.
6. Tyler told him/Harry to make his bed on weekdays.
7. Tyler said not to eat his/Tyler's food.
8. Tyler told him/Harry to be a better roommate.

2 Reported speech: statements
1. Lori said (that) she had to visit her grandparents that day. Lori told them (that) she had to visit her grandparents that day.
2. Mario said/told them (that) he was going to a play on Sunday.
3. Julia said/told them (that) she had promised to take her brother to the movies that day.
4. Daniel said/told them (that) he couldn't come because he had to study for a huge exam on Monday.
5. The neighbors said/told them (that) they would be out of town all weekend.
6. Alice said/told them (that) she might have to babysit her nephew.

Credits

The authors and publishers acknowledge the following sources of copyright material and are grateful for the permissions granted. While every effort has been made, it has not always been possible to identify the sources of all the material used, or to trace all copyright holders. If any omissions are brought to our notice, we will be happy to include the appropriate acknowledgements on reprinting and in the next update to the digital edition, as applicable.

Texts

Text on p. 13 adapted from "The 4 Happiest Cities on Earth" by Ford Cochran. Copyright © National Geographic Creative. Reproduced with permission; Mark Boyle for the text on p. 21 adapted from "Living without money changed my way of being." Reproduced with kind permission of Mark Boyle; Text on p. 41 adapted from "World's weirdest hotel requests and complaints" by James Teideman. Copyright © www.skyscanner.net. Reproduced with kind permission; Text on p. 83 adapted from "Deaf band 'Beethoven's Nightmare' feels the music" by Dennis McCarthy. Copyright © Los Angeles Daily News. Reproduced with permission.

Key: B = Below, BC = Below Centre, BL = Below Left, BR = Below Right, B/G = Background, C = Centre, CL = Centre Left, CR = Centre Right, L = Left, R = Right, T = Top, TC = Top Centre, TL = Top Left, TR = Top Right.

Illustrations

337 Jon (KJA Artists): 39, 92(B), 97; **Mark Duffin**: 18, 25(C), 37, 43(T); **Pablo Gallego** (Beehive Illustration): 43(B); **Thomas Girard** (Good Illustration): 2, 22, 41, 93; **John Goodwin** (Eye Candy Illustration): 40; **Daniel Gray**: 75, 118, 120; **Quino Marin** (The Organisation): 36, 80, 128; **Gavin Reece** (New Division): 58, 81, 119; **Paul Williams** (Sylvie Poggio Artists): 16, 114.

Photos

Back cover (woman with whiteboard): Jenny Acheson/Stockbyte/GettyImages; Back cover (whiteboard): Nemida/GettyImages; Back cover (man using phone): Betsie Van Der Meer/Taxi/GettyImages; Back cover (woman smiling): PeopleImages.com/DigitalVision/GettyImages; Back cover (name tag): Tetra Images/GettyImages; Back cover (handshake): David Lees/Taxi/Getty Images; p. v (TL): Hero Images/Getty Images; p. v (TR): Cultura RM Exclusive/dotdotred/Getty Images; p. v (CL): vitchanan/iStock/Getty Images Plus/Getty Images; p. v (CR): Svetlana Braun/iStock/Getty Images Plus/Getty Images; p. v (BL): Hero Images/Getty Images; p. v (BR): Cultura RM Exclusive/dotdotred/Getty Images; p. vi (Unit 1), p. 2 (header): Ekaterina Borner/Moment Open/Getty Images; p. 2 (TL): Juanmonino/E+/Getty Images; p. 2 (TR): Purestock/Getty Images; p. 6 (TR): GlobalStock/E+/Getty Images; p. 5 (TL): JGI/Jamie Grill/Blend Images/Getty Images; p. 5 (T): Maskot/Maskot/Getty Images; p. 6 (CL): Alistair Berg/DigitalVision/Getty Images; p. 7 (TL): Bettmann/Getty Images; p. 7 (BR): Alberto Pizzoli/AFP/Getty Images; p. vi (Unit 2), p. 8 (header): Ekaterina Borner/Maskot/Getty Images; p. 8 (traffic jam): Roevin/Moment/Getty Images; p. 8 (green space): Yutthana Jantong/EyeEm/Getty Images; p. 8 (Ex 2a.a): Sergiy Serdyuk/Hemera/Getty Images Plus/Getty Images; p. 8 (Ex 2a.b): AvalancheZ/iStock/Getty Images Plus/Getty Images; p. 8 (Ex 2a.c): Peeterv/iStock/Getty Images Plus/Getty Images; p. 8 (microphone): Darryn van der Walt/Moment/Getty Images; p. 9: Kentaroo Tryman/Maskot/Getty Images; p. 10: arnaudbertrande/RooM/Getty Images; p. 11: Tim Bieber/Photodisc/Getty Images; p. 13 (photo 1): peder77/iStock/Getty Images Plus/Getty Images; p. 13 (photo 2): Sollina Images/The Image Bank/Getty Images; p. 13 (photo 3): Caiaimage/Paul Bradbury/Getty Images; p. 13 (photo 4): Jonathan Drake/Bloomberg/Getty Images; p. 14: Three Lions/Stringer/Getty Images; p. 15: Mark Edward Atkinson/Blend Images/Getty Images; p. vi (Unit 3), p. 16 (header): Hill Street Studios/Blend Images/Getty Images; p. 16 (BR): Lihee Avidan/Photonica World/Getty Images; p. 17 (L): Leren Lu/Taxi Japan/Getty Images; p. 17 (R): Aliyev Alexei Sergeevich/Blend Images/Getty Images; p. 18: Coneyl Jay/Stockbyte/Getty Images; p. 19 (T): laflor/iStock/Getty Images Plus/Getty Images; p. 19 (B): Westend61/Getty Images; p. 20: Jose Luis Pelaez Inc/Blend Images/Getty Images; p. 21: © Mark Boyle; p. vi (Unit 4), p. 22 (header): Yuri_Arcurs/DigitalVision/Getty Images; p. 22 (L): Anna Pustynnikova/iStock/Getty Images Plus/Getty Images; p. 22 (CL): John Ibarra Photography/Moment/Getty Images; p. 22 (CR): PuspaSwara/iStock/Getty Images Plus/Getty Images; p. 22 (R): trindade51/iStock/Getty Images Plus/Getty Images; p. 22 (B): Dan Dalton/DigitalVision/Getty Images; p. 23: Dan Stuart/Getty Images; p. 24 (TR): bdspn/iStock/Getty Images Plus/Getty Images; p. 24 (bake): Mark_KA/iStock/Getty Images Plus/Getty Images; p. 24 (boil): Dorling Kindersley/Getty Images; p. 24 (fry): Chris Everard/The Image Bank/Getty Images; p. 24 (grill): Dave Bradley Photography/The Image Bank/Getty Images; p. 24 (roast): Lew Robertson/Photographer's Choice/Getty Images; p. 24 (steam): Aberration Films Ltd/Science Photo Library/Getty Images; p. 25 (TR): Lauri Patterson/E+/Getty Images; p. 25 (photo 1): Simon Wheeler Ltd/Photolibrary/Getty Images; p. 25 (photo 2): jacktherabbit/iStock/Getty Images Plus/Getty Images; p. 25 (photo 3): Dave King/Dorling Kindersley/Getty Images; p. 25 (photo 4): Bruce James/StockFood Creative/Getty Images; p. 25 (photo 5): robdoss/iStock/Getty Images Plus/Getty Images; p. 26 (spaghetti): Lauri Patterson/E+/Getty Images; p. 26 (cookies): 4kodiak/E+/Getty Images; p. 26 (salsa): Douglas Johns/StockFood Creative/Getty Images; p. 26 (toast): DebbiSmirnoff/iStock/Getty Images Plus/Getty Images; p. 26 (popcorn): Michael Deuson/Photolibrary/Getty Images; p. 26 (CR): Plattform/Getty Images; p. 26 (BL): AD077/iStock/Getty Images Plus/Getty Images; p. 27 (TR): stevecoleimages/E+/Getty Images; p. 27 (BL): Lombardis Pizza of New York City; p. 29 (CR): Lauri Patterson/E+/Getty Images; p. 29 (BR): Echo/Cultura/Getty Images; p. vi (Unit 5), p. 30 (header): Hero Images/Getty Images; p. 30 (Ex 1: photo 1): Gary John Norman/Cultura Exclusive/Getty Images; p. 30 (Ex 1: photo 2): Yuri_Arcurs/DigitalVision/Getty Images; p. 30 (Ex 1: photo 3): LuckyBusiness/iStock/Getty Images Plus/Getty Images; p. 30 (Ex 1: photo 4): Yellow Dog Productions/The Image Bank/Getty Images; p. 30 (BR): AID/a.collectionRF/Getty Images; p. 31: Ed Freeman/The Image Bank/Getty Images; p. 33: AngiePhotos/E+/Getty Images; p. 34 (CR): John W Banagan/Photographer's Choice/Getty Images; p. 34 (BR): annebaek/iStock/Getty Images Plus/Getty Images; p. 35 (photo 1): Brian Bailey/The Image Bank/Getty Images; p. 35 (photo 2): Matteo Colombo/Moment/Getty Images; p. 35 (photo 3): Adam Woolfitt/robertharding/Getty Images; p. vi (Unit 6), p. 36 (header): B and G Images/Photographer's Choice/Getty Images; p. 36 (TL): Westend61/Getty Images; p. 38 (CR): Stockbyte/Getty Images; p. 38 (BR): DragonImages/iStock/Getty Images Plus/Getty Images; p. 42: Rudi Von Briel/Photolibrary/Getty Images; p. vi (Unit 7), p. 44 (header): anyaivanova/iStock/Getty Images Plus/Getty Images; p. 44 (TR): MixAll Studio/Blend Images/Getty Images; p. 45: monkeybusinessimages/iStock/Getty Images Plus/Getty Images; p. 46 (CR): scyther5/iStock/Getty Images Plus/Getty Images; p. 46 (BR): Michele Falzone/AWL Images/Getty Images; p. 47: Maskot/Maskot/Getty Images; p. 48 (speaker): Atsadej0819/iStock/Getty Images Plus/Getty Images; p. 48 (GPS): Peter Dazeley/Photographer's Choice/Getty Images; p. 48 (flash drive): Westend61/Getty Images; p. 48 (smartphone): milindri/iStock/Getty Images Plus/Getty Images; p. 48 (ATM): Volodymyr Krasyuk/iStock/Getty Images Plus/Getty Images; p. 49: Daren Woodward/iStock/Getty Images Plus/Getty Images; p. vi (Unit 8), p. 50 (header): ferrantraite/E+/Getty Images; p. 50 (Saint Patrick's Day): Sachin Polassery/Moment Editorial/Getty Images; p. 50 (Day of the Dead): Darryl Leniuk/Photographer's Choice/Getty Images; p. 50 (Chinese New year): WILLIAM WEST/AFP/Getty Images; p. 50 (Thanksgiving): Kathryn Russell Studios/Photolibrary/Getty Images; p. 51 (L): Hero Images/Getty Images; p. 51 (C): JGI/Jamie Grill/Blend Images/Getty Images; p. 51 (R): Blend Images – JGI/Jamie Grill/Brand X Pictures/Getty Images; p. 52 (TL): altrendo images/Getty Images; p. 52 (CR): Thinkstock Images/Stockbyte/Getty Images; p. 52 (B): huzu1959/Moment Open/Getty Images; p. 53 (Julia): Tara Moore/Stone/Getty Images; p. 53 (Anusha): Carlina Teteris/Moment/Getty Images; p. 53 (TR): Blend Images/Getty Images; p. 54: Tetra Images/Getty Images; p. 55 (TL): oversnap/iStock/Getty Images Plus/Getty Images; p. 55 (BR): ruslan117/iStock/Getty Images Plus/Getty Images; p. 56 (CR): vgajic/iStock/Getty Images Plus/Getty Images; p. 57 (TL): Dezein/iStock/Getty Images Plus/Getty Images; p. 57 (TC): artpartner-images/Photographer's Choice/Getty Images; p. 57 (TR): André Rieck/EyeEmGetty Images; p. 57 (BR): Satoshi Kawase/Moment/Getty Images; p. vi (Unit 9), p. 58 (header): Artur Debat/Moment/Getty Images; p. 58 (TL): Michael Fresco/Evening Standard/Hulton Archive/Getty Images; p. 58 (TC): Car Culture/Car Culture ® Collection/Getty Images; p. 58 (TR): Javier Pierini/The Image Bank/Getty Images; p. 59: Hero Images/Getty Images; p. 60 (CR): Jordan Siemens/Iconica/Getty Images; p. 60 (BR): RoBeDeRo/E+/Getty Images; p. 61: GH-Photography/iStock/Getty Images Plus/Getty Images; p. 62 (TR): Barry Austin Photography/Iconica/Getty Images; p. 62 (Ex 11a: photo 1): Hill Street Studios/Blend Images/Getty Images; p. 62 (Ex 11a: photo 2): Hill Street Studios/Blend Images/Getty Images; p. 62 (Ex 11a: photo 3): Hill Street Studios/Blend Images/Getty Images; p. 62 (Ex 11a: photo 4): Aziz Ary Neto/Cultura/Getty Images; p. 62 (Ex 11a: photo 5): Blend Images-Mike Kemp/Brand X Pictures/Getty Images; p. 63: Daniel Schoenen/LOOK-foto/LOOK/Getty Images; p. vi (Unit 10), p. 64 (header): Hero Images/Getty Images; p. 64 (BR): BJI/Blue Jean Images/Getty Images; p. 65: Caiaimage/Paul Bradbury/Caiaimage/Getty Images; p. 67 (disorganised): Stuart McCall/Photographer's Choice/Getty Images; p. 67 (hardworking): Dave and Les Jacobs/Blend Images/Getty Images; p. 67 (Ex 9a): adventtr/E+/Getty Images; p. 67 (Paula): Portra Images/Taxi/Getty Images; p. 67 (Shawn): PeopleImages/DigitalVision/Getty Images; p. 67 (Dalia): Jetta Productions/Blend Images/Getty Images; p. 68: Hill Street Studios/Getty Images; p. 69: Image Source/Getty Images; p. 71: monkeybusinessimages/iStock/Getty Images Plus/Getty Images; p. vi (Unit 11), p. 72 (header): d3sign/Moment/Getty Images; p. 72 (Eiffel Tower): Kart Thomas/Photolibrary/Getty Images; p. 72 (Machu Picchu): mimmopellicola.com/Moment/Getty Images; p. 72 (Neuschwanstein Castle): Brian Lawrence/Getty Images; p. 72 (Mount Fuji): Christian Kober/robertharding/Getty Images; p. 72 (Statue of Liberty): Brian Lawrence/Getty Images; p. 72 (Big Ben): Joe Fox/Photographer's Choice/Getty Images; p. 73: Print Collector/Hulton Fine Art Collection/Getty Images; p. 74 (L): JTB Photo/Universal Images Group/Getty Images; p. 74 (C): PIERRE VERDY/AFP Creative/Getty Images; p. 74 (R): JLGutierrez/iStock/Getty Images Plus/Getty Images; p. 76: Radius Images/Getty Images Plus/Getty Images; p. 76 (CR): Jodi Jacobson/E+/Getty Images; p. 76 (BR): Photography Aubrey Stoll/Moment/Getty Images; p. 77: Hemant Chawla/The India Today Group/Getty Images; p. 77 (CR): Luis Javier Sandoval/Oxford Scientific/Getty Images; p. 77 (BL): EPA european pressphoto agency b.v./Alamy; p. vi (Unit 12), p. 78 (header): Timur Emek/Getty Images Europe/Getty Images; p. 78 (TL): JasnaXX/RooM/Getty Images; p. 78 (TR): Rodrigo Alvarez-Icaza/Moment Open/Getty Images; p. 78 (BR): James Woodson/Photodisc/Getty Images; p. 79 (TR): Michael Krinke/Vetta/Getty Images; p. 79 (BR): biglike/iStock/Getty Images Plus/Getty Images; p. 82: David Lees/Taxi/Getty Images; p. 83: Rachel Murray/WireImage/Getty Images; p. 84: Ben Pruchnie/Getty Images Europe/Getty Images; p. vi (Unit 13), p. 86 (header): spawns/iStock/Getty Images Plus/Getty Images; p. 86 (TL): Jim Spellman/WireImage/Getty Images; p. 86 (TR): Pictorial Press Ltd/Alamy; p. 86 (BR): Murray Close/Contributor/Moviepix/GettyImages; p. 87: Araya Diaz/WireImage/Getty Image; p. 89: Jon Kopaloff/FilmMagic/Getty Images; p. 90 (TR): Daniel Zuchnik/WireImage/Getty Images; p. 90 (BR): Valerie Macon/Getty Images North America/Getty Images; p. 91 (BL): Paul Hawthorne/Getty Images North America/Getty Images; p. 91 (TR): Alberto E. Rodriguez/Getty Images North America/Getty Images; p. vi (Unit 14), p. 92 (header): Joe Drivas/Photographer's Choice/Getty Images; p. 93 (Ex 4: photo 1): champja/iStock/Getty Images Plus/Getty Images; p. 93 (Ex 4: photo 2): Dahl Per/Getty Images; p. 93 (Ex 4: photo 3): Seymour Hewitt/The Image Bank/Getty Images; p. 93 (Ex 4: photo 4): Merbe/E+/Getty Images; p. 93 (Ex 4: photo 5): BJI/Blue Jean Images/Getty Images; p. 93 (Ex 4: photo 6): m-imagephotography/iStock/Getty Images Plus/Getty Images; p. 94: BJI/Blue Jean Images/Getty Images; p. 98: uniquely india/Getty Images; p. 99: GlobalStock/E+/Getty Images; p. vi (Unit 15), p. 100 (header): Tetra Images/Getty Images; p. 100 (TL): moodboard/Brand X Pictures/Getty Images; p. 100 (CL): Marcin Balcerzak/Hemera/Getty Images Plus/Getty Images; p. 100 (C): Erik Dreyer/The Image Bank/Getty Images; p. 100 (BR): Thomas_EyeDesign/E+/Getty Images; p. 102: pp76/iStock/Getty Images Plus/Getty Images; p. 104 (TR): Wavebreakmedia Ltd/Wavebreak Media/Getty Images Plus/Getty Images; p. 104 (CR): Ariel Skelley/Blend Images/Getty Images Plus/Getty Images; p. 105 (Jack): Frank Herholdt/The Image Bank/Getty Images; p. 105 (Sarah): Betsie Van Der Meer/Taxi/Getty Images; p. 105 (Maya): Caiaimage/Sam Edwards/Caiaimage/Getty Images; p. 105 (Dag): Dimitri Otis/Taxi/Getty Images; p. 105 (Andres): Ridofranz/iStock/Getty Images Plus/Getty Images; p. 105 (Marta): Mark Edward Atkinson/Tracey Lee/Blend Images/Getty Images; p. vi (Unit 16), p. 106 (header): Dan Dumitru Comaniciu/iStock/Getty Images Plus/Getty Images; p. 106 (TR): GK Hart/Vikki Hart/Stone/Getty Images; p. 107: ajr_images/iStock/Getty Images Plus/Getty Images; p. 108 (Gabriel): gradyreese/E+/Getty Images; p. 108 (Craig): Leland Bobbe/Image Source/Getty Images; p. 109 (Grant): Ezra Bailey/Taxi/Getty Images; p. 109 (Sayo): Sappington Todd/Getty Images; p. 109 (Carrie): Jordan Siemens/Getty Images; p. 109 (Jack): Fuse/Getty Images; p. 110: Jamie Grill/Photodisc/Getty Images; p. 111 (TR): Tom Le Goff/DigitalVision/Getty Images; p. 111 (CR): Ugurhan Betin/iStock/Getty Images Plus/Getty Images; p. 112:

Moodboard Stock Photography Ltd./Canopy/Getty Images; p. 115 (TL): DC_Colombia/iStock/Getty Images Plus/Getty Images; p. 115 (TR): Rob Carr/Getty Images; p. 115 (BL): Sylvester Adams/DigitalVision/Getty Images; p. 115 (BR): 9Tiw/iStock/Getty Images Plus/Getty Images; p. 116: Paul Burns/DigitalVision/Getty Images; p. 117: Jon Feingersh/Blend Images/Getty Images; p. 118: Vince Cavataio/Design Pics/Perspectives/Getty Images; p. 120: Michele Falzone/Photographer's Choice/Getty Images; p. 121 (TL): Yellow Dog Productions/The Image Bank/Getty Images; p. 121 (TR): Klaus Vedfelt/DigitalVision/Getty Images; p. 121 (CL): Susan Chiang/E+/Getty Images; p. 121 (CR): Nick White and Fiona Jackson-Downes/Cultura/Getty Images; p. 121 (BL): Steve Debenport/iStock/Getty Images Plus/Getty Images; p. 121 (BR): Celia Peterson/arabianEye/Getty Images; p. 122 (BL): Jon Feingersh/Blend Images/Getty Images; p. 122 (BC): Blend Images-Jose Luis Pelaez Inc/Brand X Pictures/Getty Images; p. 122 (BR): Westend61/Getty Images; p. 123 (Ex a.1): Hero Images/Getty Images; p. 123 (Ex a.2): Kontrec/E+/Getty Images; p. 123 (Ex a.3): Robert Daly/Caiaimage/Getty Images; p. 123 (Ex a.4): quavondo/E+/Getty Images; p. 123 (Ex a.5): Wavebreakmedia Ltd/Wavebreak Media/Getty Images Plus/Getty Images; p. 123 (Ex a.6): Wendy Connett/Moment/Getty Images; p. 123 (Ex a.7): Dimitri Otis/DigitalVision/Getty Images; p. 123 (Ex a.8): Justin Pumfrey/Iconica/Getty Images; p. 123 (Ex a.9): monkeybusinessimages/iStock/Getty Images Plus/Getty Images; p. 123 (Ex a.10): Alberto Guglielmi/The Image Bank/Getty Images; p. 124: opolja/iStock/Getty Images Plus/Getty Images; p. 125 (B/G): CSA Images/Printstock Collection/Getty Images; p. 126 (TL): blackred/E+/Getty Images; p. 126 (TR): blackred/E+/Getty Images; p. 126 (B/G): Nathaniel Newbold/EyeEm/Getty Images; p. 127: JGI/Tom Grill/Blend Images/Getty Images; p. 130: Joos Mind/Taxi/Getty Images.